LIST OF CONTENTS

INTRODUCTION   Page 2

ORGANISATION TABLES   Pages 4 – 9

CAMPAIGN SUMMARY   Page 10

DIVISIONS   Pages 11 – 79

EQUIPMENT
     TANKS   Page 80
     ARMD VEHICLES   Page 81
     SP GUNS   Page 81
     GUN PERFORMANCE   Page 82

VEHICLE COLOURS   Page 83

MARKINGS & INSIGNIA
     SHOULDER PATCH   (see DIVISIONS)
     NATIONAL MARKINGS   Page 84
     BUMPER CODES   Page 85
     ARMD DIVISIONS   Page 86
     SERIAL NUMBERS   Page 87
     BRIDGE NUMBERS   Page 87
     RANK INSIGNIA   Page 87

INDEX TO DIVISIONS AND
    COMPONENT UNITS   Pages 88 – 90

SELECT BIBLIOGRAPHY   Page 90

FRONT COVER

M2 Half-Track Personnel Carrier

(RAC Museum)

U.S. DIVISIONS - N.AFRICA & EUROPE 1942-45

INTRODUCTION

This book continues with the objectives of the Datafile Series, attempting to reduce time spent on research by collating data on organisation, component units, dispositions, insignia and markings.

U.S. Divisions first entered combat in the West with the landings in North Africa (Operation Torch), November 1942. At no time did the U.S. presence in the Mediterranean Theatre (Tunisia, Sicily, Italy, Southern France) exceed seven Infantry, one Armored and one Airborne Division. By comparison, in Central Europe 1945, no less than forty Infantry, fifteen Armored and four Airborne Divisions were deployed, representing a significant proportion of Allied combat troops engaged in the operations for the liberation of Europe.

U.S. Divisions were roughly the equivalent of their British or German counterparts with 14,000 personnel (Infantry), 13,000 (Airborne) and 11,000 (Armored). Divisional commanders were usually of the rank of Major General, branches of the division (Combat Commands, Artillery etc) were commanded by a Brigadier General and individual Regiments or battalions by a Lieutenant Colonel, although some variation did occur in practice.

Unlike British or German Divisions, no divisional insignia was displayed on the vehicles and regimental insignia was forbidden in combat areas. The insignia illustrated in this book represent those worn on uniform shoulders. A 'bumper-code' was prescribed for vehicle marking, the significance of these being explained in the text.

The included organisation charts have been slightly simplified for clarity, some support and headquarters units being ommitted. The charts should, however, give a good indication of unit organisation.

Thanks are extended to those enthusiasts who have commented and advised on the Datafile Books, and I look forward to their reactions and criticisms of the latest, Datafile 6

S.75
NN

U.S. DIVISIONS – N. AFRICA & EUROPE

1942-45

Compiled and published by:-

Mr. MALCOLM A. BELLIS
10 WHITE HART LANE
WISTASTON, CREWE
CHESHIRE, CW2 8EX

THE DATAFILE SERIES

DATAFILE 1 (2nd Edition)

'British Tanks & Formations 1939-45'
ISBN 0 9512126 2 1

DATAFILE 2

'Divisions of the British Army 1939-45'
ISBN 0 9512126 0 5

DATAFILE 3

'Brigades of the British Army 1939-45'
ISBN 0 9512126 1 3

DATAFILE 4

'German Tanks & Formations 1939-45'
ISBN 0 9512126 4 8

DATAFILE 5

'British Armoured & Infantry
                        Regiments 1939-45'
ISBN 0 9512126 3 X

DIVISIONAL TABLES OF ORGANISATION - KEY TO ABREVIATIONS

Unless otherwise stated these TOA apply at September 1943. The 1942 TOA differ for some of the units prescribed.

AA	Anti-Aircraft	HMG	Heavy Machine Gun	Para	Parachute
Admin	Administration	HQ	Headquarters	Pers	Personnel
AM&S	Admin, Mess & Supply	Howz	Howitzer	Pl	Platoon
Amb	Ambulance	Hy	Heavy	pwr	power
Ammo	Ammunition	HyWk	Heavy Wrecker		
Arm	Armament			QM	Quartermaster
Arty	Artillery	Inf	Infantry		
Armd	Armored	Insp	Inspection	RCT	Regt Combat Team
ARV	Armd Recovery Vehicle	Instm	Instrument	Regt	Regiment
Asslt	Assault	Intel	Intelligence	Recce	Reconnaissance
ATk	Anti-Tank	Lt	Light	Rif	Rifle (M1/M1903)
Auto	Automatic	LMG	Light Machine Gun	S/Arm	Small Arms
				Sec	Section
BAR	Browning Auto Rifle	Maint	Maintenance	Sigs	Signals
Bty	Battery	Mech	Mechanical	Sqd	Squad
Bdge	Bridge (ing)	Med	Medium	Sqn	Squadron
Bn	Battalion	Medic	Medical	SP	Self-Propelled
Bazk	Bazooka	Mes	Message	Supp	Support
		Met	Meteorological		
Cav	Cavalry	MG	Machine Gun	Ŧ	Trailer
Chem	Chemical	Mort	Mortar	TD	Tank Destroyer
Comm	Communications	Mot	Motorised	Tk	Tank
Commd	Command	MP	Military Police	Tp	Troop
Compr	Compressor			Trac	Tractor
Coy	Company	M3*	Half-Track	Trk	Truck (or ¼t, 2½t etc)
Ctr	Center	M8*	Greyhound Armd Car	Trans	Transport
		M7*	105mm SP Howitzer		
Divn	Division	M10*	Ammunition Trailer	Wire	Wireless
		M21*	Half-Track (81mm Mort)	Wksp	Workshop
Engr	Engineer			Wpns	Weapons
Exec	Executive	Obs	Observation		
		Ops	Operations		
Fld	Field	Ord	Ordnance		
Fwd	Forward				

* For fuller list of designations see 'Equipment'

ARMORED DIVISION

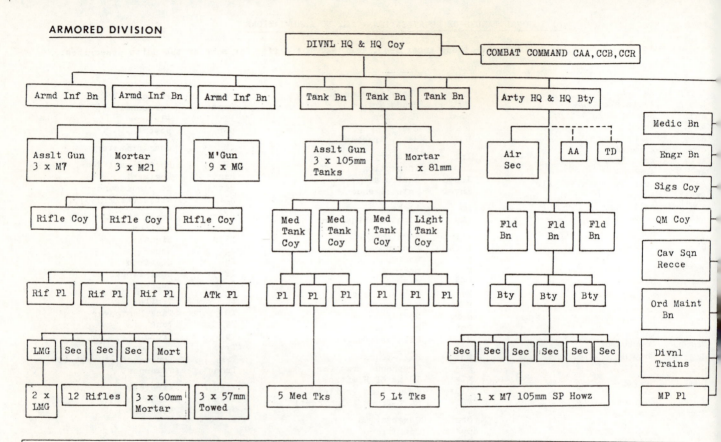

Notes : M21 - M3 Half-Track with 81mm Mortar
M7 - 105mm Howitzer on Lee chassis
57mm - Towed A'Tank gun based on British 6pdr
Medium Tank - M4 Sherman, Light Tank M3/M5 Stuart
AA (Anti-Aircraft) & TD (Tank-Destroyer) Bns
attached from Corps or Army Troops

INFANTRY DIVISION

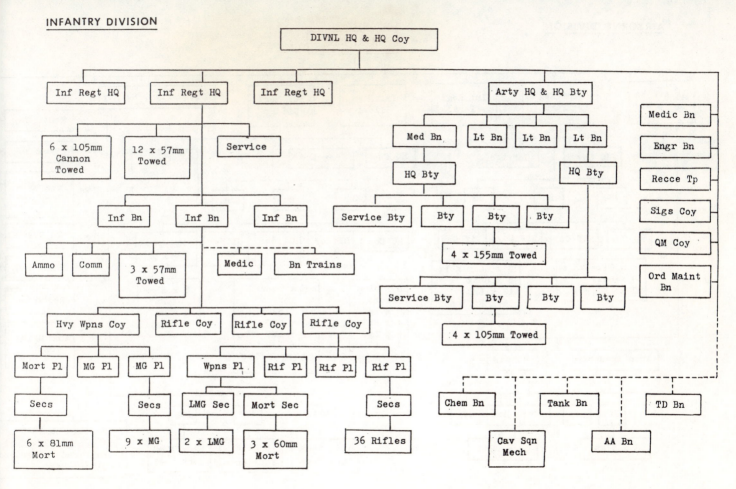

AIRBORNE DIVISION

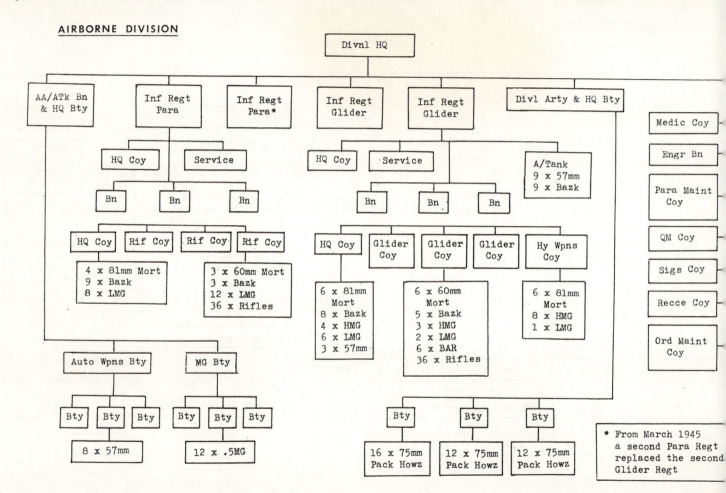

ORDNANCE MAINTENANCE BATTALION

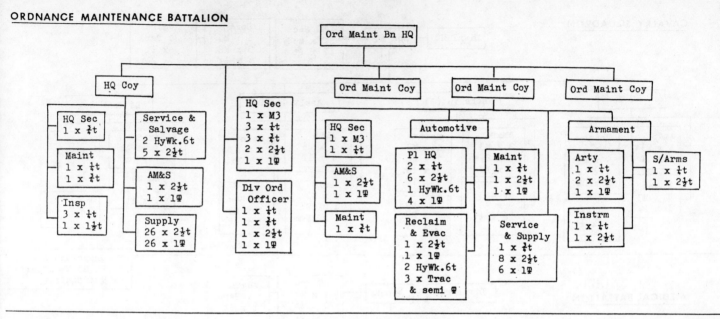

REGIMENTAL COMBAT TEAM

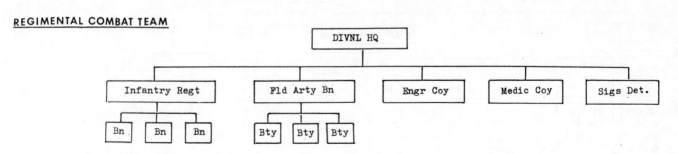

CAVALRY SQUADRON

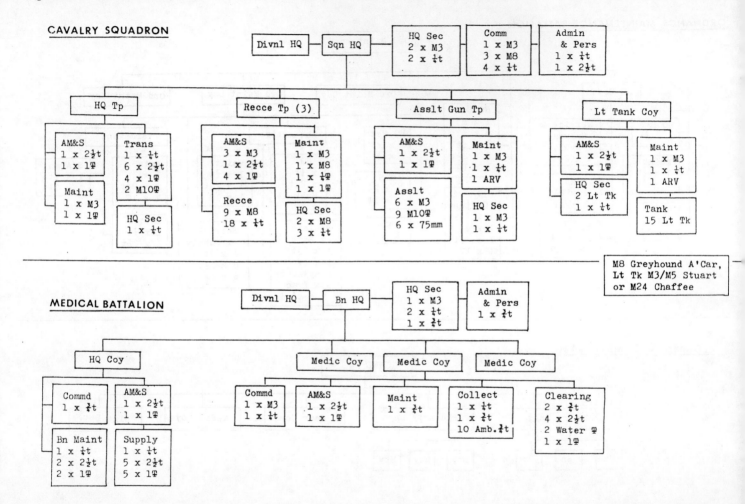

| Divnl HQ | Sqn HQ |

HQ Sec
2 x M3
2 x ¼t

Comm
1 x M3
3 x M8
4 x ¼t

Admin
& Pers
1 x ¼t
1 x 2½t

HQ Tp

AM&S
1 x 2½t
1 x 1⊤

Trans
1 x ¼t
6 x 2½t
4 x 1⊤
2 M10⊤

Maint
1 x M3
1 x 1⊤

HQ Sec
1 x ¼t

Recce Tp (3)

AM&S
3 x M3
1 x 2½t
4 x 1⊤

Maint
1 x M3
1 x M8
1 x ¼⊤
1 x 1⊤

Recce
9 x M8
18 x ¼t

HQ Sec
2 x M8
3 x ¼t

Asslt Gun Tp

AM&S
1 x 2½t
1 x 1⊤

Maint
1 x M3
1 x ¼t
1 ARV

Asslt
6 x M3
9 M10⊤
6 x 75mm

HQ Sec
1 x M3
1 x ¼t

Lt Tank Coy

AM&S
1 x 2½t
1 x 1⊤

Maint
1 x M3
1 x ¼t
1 ARV

HQ Sec
2 Lt Tk
1 x ¼t

Tank
15 Lt Tk

M8 Greyhound A'Car,
Lt Tk M3/M5 Stuart
or M24 Chaffee

MEDICAL BATTALION

| Divnl HQ | Bn HQ |

HQ Sec
1 x M3
2 x ¼t
1 x ¾t

Admin
& Pers
1 x ¾t

HQ Coy

Commd
1 x ¾t

AM&S
1 x 2½t
1 x 1⊤

Bn Maint
1 x ¼t
2 x 2½t
2 x 1⊤

Supply
1 x ¼t
5 x 2½t
5 x 1⊤

Medic Coy   **Medic Coy**   **Medic Coy**

Commd
1 x M3
1 x ¼t

AM&S
1 x 2½t
1 x 1⊤

Maint
1 x ¾t

Collect
1 x ¼t
1 x ¾t
10 Amb.¾t

Clearing
2 x ¾t
4 x 2½t
2 Water ⊤
1 x 1⊤

ENGINEER BATTALION

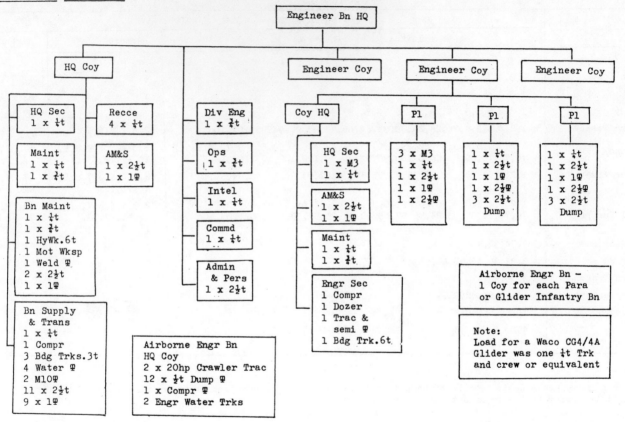

Engineer Bn HQ

HQ Coy

HQ Sec
1 x ¼t

Maint
1 x ¼t
1 x ¾t

Bn Maint
1 x ¼t
1 x ¾t
1 HyWk.6t
1 Mot Wksp
1 Weld ☗
2 x 2½t
1 x 1☗

Bn Supply & Trans
1 x ¼t
1 Compr
3 Bdg Trks.3t
4 Water ☗
2 M10☗
11 x 2½t
9 x 1☗

Recce
4 x ¼t

AM&S
1 x 2½t
1 x 1☗

Div Eng
1 x ¾t

Ops
1 x ¾t

Intel
1 x ¼t

Commd
1 x ¼t

Admin & Pers
1 x 2½t

Engineer Coy

Coy HQ

HQ Sec
1 x M3
1 x ¼t

AM&S
1 x 2½t
1 x 1☗

Maint
1 x ¼t
1 x ¾t

Engr Sec
1 Compr
1 Dozer
1 Trac & semi ☗
1 Bdg Trk.6t

Pl
3 x M3
1 x ¼t
1 x 2½t
1 x 1☗
1 x 2½☗

Engineer Coy

Pl
1 x ¼t
1 x 2½t
1 x 1☗
1 x 2½☗
3 x 2½t
Dump

Engineer Coy

Pl
1 x ¼t
1 x 2½t
1 x 1☗
1 x 2½☗
3 x 2½t
Dump

Airborne Engr Bn —
1 Coy for each Para
or Glider Infantry Bn

Note:
Load for a Waco CG4/4A
Glider was one ¼t Trk
and crew or equivalent

Airborne Engr Bn
HQ Coy
2 x 20hp Crawler Trac
12 x ½t Dump ☗
1 x Compr ☗
2 Engr Water Trks

Campaigns	Divisions		
	Infantry	Armored	Airborne
Algeria/Morocco	1,9		
Tunisia	1,3,9,34	1	
Sicily	1,3,9,45	2	82
Normandy	1,2,4,5,8,9,28,29,30,35,79,80,83,90	2,3,4,5,6	82,101
Northern France	1,2,4,5,8,9,26,28,29,30,35,44,66,79,83,90,94,95,104,106	2,3,4,5,6,7	
Rhineland	1,2,3,4,5,8,9,26,28,29, 30,35,36,42,44,45,63,65,69,70,71,75, 76,78,79,80,83,84,87,89,90,94,95,99,100,102,103,104,106	2,3,4,5,6,7,8,9, 10,11,12,13,14	17,82,101
Ardennes/Alsace	1,2,4,5,9,26,28,30,35,45,75,76,78,80,83,84,87,90,94,99,100, 106	2,3,4,5,6,7,8,9, 10,11,12	17,82,101
Central Europe	1,2,3,4,5,8,9,26,28,29,30,35,36,42,44,45,63,65,69,70,71,75, 76,78,79,80,83,84,86,87,89,90,94,95,97,99,100,102,103,104	2,3,4,5,6,7,8,9, 10,11,12,13,14, 16,20	13,17,82,101
Naples/Fogia	3,34,36,45	1	82
Rome/Arno	3,34,36,45,85,88,91	1	82
Southern France	3,36,45		1 Task Force
North Appenines	10,34,85,88,91,92	1	
Po Valley	10,34,85,88,91,92	1	
Anzio	45		

This summary gives basic details of campaigns for each division. For further information on locations and dates refer to the individual division history.

1st AIRBORNE TASK FORCE

Of approximate divisional strength, this formation was employed for the invasion of Southern France, August 1944. Under command VI Corps, US 5th Army the force was formed in Italy.

OPERATION 'DRAGOON'

517th Parachute Infantry Regiment

    attached :   460th Parachute Field Artillery Bn
                      596th Parachute Engineer Coy
                      Anti-Tank Pln - 442nd Infantry Regiment
                      D Coy, 83rd Chemical Mortar Bn

509th Parachute Infantry Bn

    attached :   463rd Parachute Field Artillery Bn

551st Parachute Infantry Bn

    attached :   one Pln - 887th Engineer Coy

550th Glider Infantry Bn

    attached :   one Pln - 887th Engineer Coy

2nd British Independent Parachute Brigade Group*

    attached :   2nd Chemical Mortar Bn
                      64th Lt Artillery Bn

Notes :   * see Datafile 3 'Brigades of the British Army 1939-45'

SHOULDER PATCH

US National Flag worn on left upper sleeve, no other special markings

13th AIRBORNE DIVISION

Activated in the U.S.A. August 1943. Moved overseas January 1945. Returned to the U.S.A. for inactivation August 1945

February 1945

88th Glider Infantry Regiment
326th Glider Infantry Regiment

515th Parachute Infantry Regiment

676th Glider Field Arty Bn
677th Glider Field Arty Bn
458th Para Field Arty Bn

153rd Airborne AA Bn

13th Para Maintenance Coy
513th Airborne Signals Coy
713th Airborne Ordnance Coy
409th Airborne Q'master Coy
222nd Airborne Medical Coy

129th Airborne Engineer Bn

March 1945

326th Glider Infantry Regiment

515th Parachute Infantry Regt
517th Parachute Infantry Regt

676th Glider Field Arty Bn
677th Glider Field Arty Bn
458th Para Field Arty Bn
460th Para Field Arty Bn

153rd Airborne AA Bn

13th Para Maintenance Coy
*513th Airborne Signals Coy
*713th Airborne Ordnance Coy
*409th Airborne Q'master Coy
222nd Airborne Medical Coy

129th Airborne Engineer Bn

A gold unicorn on a blue shield, 'AIRBORNE' in white on black flash above

Under command 1st Allied Airborne Army. Stationed in France, not committed to action

Notes :   * u/commd HQ Special Troops from 3.45, previously u/commd Divn

17th AIRBORNE DIVISION

Activated in the U.S.A. April 1943. Moved overseas August 1944. Returned to the U.S.A. for inactivation September 1945

SHOULDER PATCH

February 1945

193rd Glider Infantry Regiment
194th Glider Infantry Regiment

513th Parachute Infantry Regiment

680th Glider Field Arty Bn
681st Glider Field Arty Bn
466th Para Field Arty Bn

155th Airborne AA Bn

17th Para Maintenance Coy
517th Airborne Signals Coy
717th Airborne Ordnance Coy
411th Airborne Q'master Coy
224th Airborne Medical Coy

139th Airborne Engineer Bn

March 1945

194th Glider Infantry Regiment

507th Parachute Infantry Regt
513th Parachute Infantry Regt

680th Glider Field Arty Bn
681st Glider Field Arty Bn
464th Para Field Arty Bn
466th Para Field Arty Bn

155th Airborne AA Bn

17th Para Maintenance Coy
* 517th Airborne Signals Coy
* 717th Airborne Ordnance Coy
* 411th Airborne Q'master Coy
224th Airborne Medical Coy

139th Airborne Engineer Bn

Gold talons on a black disc 'AIRBORNE' in white on a black flash above

UK (8.44), France, Mourmelon, Meuse, Verdun (12.44), Belgium, Morhet, Ardennes (1.45), Houffalize, Luxembourg, Seigfried Line (1.45), France (2.45), Wesel, Issel (3.45), Munster, Essen, Mulheim, Duisburg (4.45)

Notes : * u/commd HQ Special Troops from 3.45, previously u/commd Divn

82nd AIRBORNE DIVISION

Activated in the U.S.A. March 1942. Designated an Airborne Division August 1942. Moved overseas April 1943. Allied Army of Occupation, Germany, May 1945

February 1945

325th Glider Infantry Regiment

504th Parachute Infantry Regt
505th Parachute Infantry Regt

319th Glider Field Arty Bn
320th Glider Field Arty Bn
376th Para Field Arty Bn
456th Para Field Arty Bn

80th Airborne AA Bn

* 82nd Airborne Signals Coy
* 782nd Airborne Ordnance Coy
* 407th Airborne Q'master Coy
307th Airborne Medical Coy

307th Airborne Engineer Bn

March 1945

as Feb 1945 with following addition :-

82nd Para Maintenance Coy

Letters 'AA' on a blue disc set within a red square, 'AIRBORNE' in white on blue flash above

Casablanca (5.43), Sicily (7.43), Tunisia (8.43), Sicily (9.43), Salerno (9.43), Naples (10.43), UK (11.43), Normandy, Carentan, St Sauveur-le-Vicompte (6.44), UK (7.44), Nijmegen (9.44), France (11.44), Ardennes (12.44), Seigfried Line, Roer (2.45), Rhine, Elbe, Mecklenburg Plain (4.45)

Notes : * u/commd HQ Special Troops from 3.45, previously u/commd Divn

101st AIRBORNE DIVISION

Activated in the U.S.A. August 1942. Moved overseas September 1943. Inactivated in Germany, June 1945

February 1945

327th Glider Infantry Regiment
401st Glider Infantry Regiment

502nd Parachute Infantry Regiment

321st Glider Field Arty Bn
907th Glider Field Arty Bn
377th Para Field Arty Bn

81st Airborne AA Bn

101st Airborne Signals Coy
801st Airborne Ordnance Coy
426th Airborne Q'master Coy
326th Airborne Medical Coy

326th Airborne Engineer Bn

March 1945

327th Glider Infantry Regiment

502nd Parachute Infantry Regt
506th Parachute Infantry Regt

321st Glider Field Arty Bn
907th Glider Field Arty Bn
377th Para Field Arty Bn
463rd Para Field Arty Bn

81st Airborne AA Bn

101st Para Maintenance Coy
* 801st Airborne Ordnance Coy
* 101st Airborne Signals Coy
* 426th Airborne Q'master Coy
326th Airborne Medical Coy

326th Airborne Engineer Bn

white eagles head, yellow beak on a black shield

'AIRBORNE' in white on a black flash

UK (9.43), Normandy, Pouppeville, St Come du Mont (6.44), UK (7.44), Holland, Vechel, Oedenrode, Eindhoven (9.44), Opheusden (10.44), France (11.44), Bastogne (12.44), Alsace, Moder River (1.45), France (2.45), Ruhr (3.45), Munchen-Gladbach (4.45), Berchtesgarten (5.45)

Notes : * u/commd HQ Special Troops from 3.45, previously u/commd Divn

1st ARMORED DIVISION

Activated in the U.S.A. July 1940. Moved overseas May 1942. Part of Allied Army of Occupation, Italy until returning to U.S.A. in April 1945.

6th Armored Infantry Bn
11th Armored Infantry Bn
14th Armored Infantry Bn

1st Tank Battalion
4th Tank Battalion
13th Tank Battalion

27th Armd Field Artillery Bn
68th Armd Field Artillery Bn
91st Armd Field Artillery Bn

81st Cavalry Reconnaissance Sqn

16th Armored Engineer Bn

47th Armored Medical Bn

123rd Armored Ordnance Bn

141st Armored Signals Company

Combat Commands A, B & R

Triangle of red over yellow/blue, black tracks, cannon and Divisional number, red lightning

Oran (11.42), Tunisia (11.42), French Morocco (5.43), Salerno (9.43), Rapido River (12.43), Mount Porchia (1.44), Anzio (1.44), Rome (6.44), Arno (9.44), Appenines (11.44), Milan (4.45), Cigliano (4.45)

Notes : previously contained 1st & 13th Armored Regiments. Re-organised in Italy to 1943 TOA in July 1944

2nd ARMORED DIVISION

Activated in the U.S.A. July 1940. Moved overseas October-December 1942. Part of the Allied Army of Occupation, Berlin, July 1945

41st Armored Regiment
63rd Armored Regiment

67th Armored Infantry Regiment

14th Armd Field Artillery Bn
78th Armd Field Artillery Bn
92nd Armd Field Artillery Bn

Combat Commands A, B & R

82nd Armored Reconnaissance Bn

17th Armored Engineer Bn

48th Armored Medical Bn

2nd Armored Ordnance Bn

142nd Armored Signals Coy

Insignia as for
1st Armored Divn
except numeral '2'
replaces '1'

Casablanca (11.42), Tunisia (1.43), Sicily (7.43), UK (11.43), Normandy (6.44), Northern France (7.44), Belgium (9.44), Geilenkirchen (9.44), Marienburg, Wurm River (11.44), Ardennes (12.44), Rhine (3.45), Elbe (4.45), Berlin (7.45)

Notes : Division not reorganised to 1943 regulations

3rd ARMORED DIVISION

Activated in the U.S.A. April 1941. In the U.K. with 1st Army November 1943. Returned to the U.S.A. July 1945 for inactivation

32nd Armored Regiment	83rd Armored Reconnaissance Bn
33rd Armored Regiment	
	23rd Armored Engineer Bn
36th Armored Infantry Regiment	45th Armored Medical Bn
	3rd Armored Ordnance Bn
54th Armd Field Artillery Bn	
67th Armd Field Artillery Bn	143rd Armored Signals Coy
391st Armd Field Artillery Bn	

Combat Commands A, B & R

Insignia as for 1st Armored Divn except numeral '3' replaces '1'

UK (11.43), Normandy (6.44), Mayenne (7.44), Falaise (8.44), Mons (8.44), Liege, Rotgen (9.44), Houffalize (1.45), Roer, Koln (3.45), Paderborn (4.45), Dessau (5.45)

Note : Division not reorganised to 1943 regulations

4th ARMORED DIVISION

Activated in the U.S.A. April 1941. Moved overseas December 1943. Returned to U.S.A. for inactivation June 1945

10th Armored Infantry Bn
51st Armored Infantry Bn
53rd Armored Infantry Bn

25th Cavalry Reconnaissance Sqn

24th Armored Engineer Bn

8th Tank Battalion
35th Tank Battalion
37th Tank Battalion

4th Armored Medical Bn

126th Armd Ordnance Bn

22nd Armd Field Artillery Bn
66th Armd Field Artillery Bn
94th Armd Field Artillery Bn

144th Armored Signals Coy

Combat Commands A, B & R

Insignia as for
1st Armored Divn
except numeral '4'
replaces '1'

UK (1.44), Normandy (6.44), Nantes (8.44), Lunneville (9.44), Chambrey (9.44), Dieuze, Bining (11.44), Bastogne (12.44), Luxembourg (2.45), Worms, Lauterbach, (3.45), Creuzburg, Saale River (4.45), Czechoslovakia, Srakonice, Pisek (5.45)

Notes :

5th ARMORED DIVISION

Activated in the U.S.A. October 1941. Moved overseas February 1944. Returned to the U.S.A. for inactivation, June 1945

15th Armored Infantry Bn	85th Cavalry Reconnaissance Sqn
46th Armored Infantry Bn	
47th Armored Infantry Bn	
	22nd Armored Engineer Bn
10th Tank Battalion	
34th Tank Battalion	75th Armored Medical Bn
81st Tank Battalion	
	127th Armored Ordnance Bn
47th Armd Field Artillery Bn	
71st Armd Field Artillery Bn	
95th Armd Field Artillery Bn	145th Armored Signals Coy

Combat Commands A, B & R

UK (2.44), Normandy (7.44), Averanches, Le Mans (8.44), Paris (8.44), Conde, Charleville-Mezieres, Luxembourg (9.44), Monschau-Hofen (10.44), Hurtgen Forest, Roer (11.44), Verviers (12.44), Rhine, Wesel (3.45), Elbe, Tangermunde (4.45), Klotze, Elbe, Dannenberg (4.45)

Notes :

SHOULDER PATCH

Insignia as for
1st Armored Divn
except numeral '5'
replaces '1'

6th ARMORED DIVISION

Activated in the U.S.A. February 1942. Moved overseas February 1944. Returned to the U.S.A. for inactivation September 1945

SHOULDER PATCH

9th Armored Infantry Bn
44th Armored Infantry Bn
50th Armored Infantry Bn

15th Tank Battalion
68th Tank Battalion
69th Tank Battalion

128th Armd Field Artillery Bn
212th Armd Field Artillery Bn
231st Armd Field Artillery Bn

Combat Commands A, B & R

86th Cavalry Reconnaissance Sqn

25th Armored Engineer Bn

76th Armored Medical Bn

128th Armored Ordnance Bn

146th Armored Signals Coy

Insignia as for
1st Armored Divn
except numeral '6'
replaces '1'

UK (2.44), Normandy (7.44), Avranches, Brest (7.44), Lorient (8.44), Nied River (11.44), Saarbrucken (11.44), Sauer River, Bastogne (12.44), Rhine, Worms (3.45), Frankfurt, Bad-Nauheim (3.45), Mulhausen (4.45), Saale River, Buchenwald, Leipzig, Rochlitz (4.45)

Notes :

7th ARMORED DIVISION

Activated in the U.S.A. March 1942. Moved overseas January 1944. Returned to the U.S.A. for inactivation October 1945

SHOULDER PATCH

23rd Armored Infantry Bn	87th Cavalry Reconnaissance Sqn
38th Armored Infantry Bn	
48th Armored Infantry Bn	
	33rd Armored Engineer Bn
17th Tank Battalion	
31st Tank Battalion	77th Armored Medical Bn
40th Tank Battalion	
	129th Armored Ordnance Bn
434th Armd Field Artillery Bn	
440th Armd Field Artillery Bn	
489th Armd Field Artillery Bn	147th Armored Signals Coy

Combat Commands A, B & R

Insignia as for 1st Armored Divn except numeral '7' replaces '1'

UK (1.44), Normandy (8.44), Chartres (8.44), Dreux, Seine River, Verdun (8.44), Moselle, Dornot, Seille River (9.44), Antwerp (10.44), Linnich, St.Vith (12.44), Belgium, Manhay (12.44), St.Vith (1.45), Rhine, Bonn (3.45), Remagen, Ruhr Pocket, Mechlenburg (4.45)

Notes :

8th ARMORED DIVISION

Activated in the U.S.A. April 1942. Moved overseas November 1944. Part of the Allied Army of Occupation, Harz Mountains, July 1945

SHOULDER PATCH

7th Armored Infantry Bn	88th Cavalry Reconnaissance Sqn
49th Armored Infantry Bn	
58th Armored Infantry Bn	
	53rd Armored Engineer Bn
18th Tank Battalion	
36th Tank Battalion	78th Armored Medical Bn
80th Tank Battalion	
	130th Armored Ordnance Bn
398th Armd Field Artillery Bn	
399th Armd Field Artillery Bn	
405th Armd Field Artillery Bn	148th Armored Signals Coy
Combat Commands A, B & R	

Insignia as for
1st Armored Divn
except numeral '8'
replaces '1'

UK (11.44), Normandy, Bacqueville (1.45), Pont-a-Mousson (1.45), Holland, Simpelveld
(2.45), Roermond, Roer River (2.45), Tetelrath, Oberkruchten, Lindfort, Rhine (3.45),
Dorsten, Lippe River, Neuhaus, Soest (3.45), Wolfenbuttel, Blankenberg, Harz Mtns (4.45)

Notes :

24

9th ARMORED DIVISION

Activated in U.S.A. July 1942. Moved overseas August 1944. Returned to the U.S.A. for inactivation October 1945

SHOULDER PATCH

27th Armored Infantry Bn
52nd Armored Infantry Bn
60th Armored Infantry Bn

89th Cavalry Reconnaissance Sqn

9th Armored Engineer Bn

2nd Tank Battalion
14th Tank Battalion
19th Tank Battalion

2nd Armored Medical Bn

131st Armored Ordnance Bn

3rd Armd Field Artillery Bn
16th Armd Field Artillery Bn
73rd Armd Field Artillery Bn

149th Armored Signals Coy

Combat Commands A, B & R

Insignia as for
1st Armored Divn
except numeral '9'
replaces '1'

Normandy (9.44), Luxembourg (10.44), St Vith, Echternach, Bastogne (12.44), Roer River, Rheinbach, Remagen (3.45), Limburg, Frankfurt (3.45), Leipzig, Mulde River (4.45), Czechoslovakia (5.45)

Notes :

10th ARMORED DIVISION

Activated in the U.S.A. July 1942. Moved overseas September 1944. Returned to the U.S.A. for inactivation October 1945

SHOULDER PATCH

20th Armored Infantry Bn
54th Armored Infantry Bn
61st Armored Infantry Bn

90th Cavalry Reconnaissance Sqn

55th Armored Engineer Bn

3rd Tank Battalion
11th Tank Battalion
21st Tank Battalion

80th Armored Medical Bn

419th Armd Field Artillery Bn
420th Armd Field Artillery Bn
423rd Armd Field Artillery Bn

132nd Armored Ordnance Bn

150th Armored Signals Coy

Combat Commands A, B & R

Insignia as for
1st Armored Divn
except numeral
'10' replaces '1'

Cherbourg (9.44), Teurtheville (10.44), Mars-la-Tour (11.44), Malling, Metz (11.44), Bastogne, Noville, Bras (12.44), Saar (1.45), Saar-Moselle (2.45), Trier, Mannheim (3.45), Oehringen, Heilbron, Kirchheim, Danube (4.45), Oberammergau, Innsbruck (5.45)

Notes :

11th ARMORED DIVISION

Activated in the U.S.A. August 1942. Moved overseas September 1944. Inactivated in Europe August 1945

21st Armored Infantry Bn
55th Armored Infantry Bn
63rd Armored Infantry Bn

41st Cavalry Reconnaissance Sqn

56th Armored Engineer Bn

22nd Tank Battalion
41st Tank Battalion
42nd Tank Battalion

81st Armored Medical Bn

133rd Armored Ordnance Bn

490th Armd Field Artillery Bn
491st Armd Field Artillery Bn
492nd Armd Field Artillery Bn

151st Armored Signals Coy

Combat Commands A, B & R

Insignia as for 1st Armored Divn except numeral '11' replaces '1'

UK (11.44), Normandy, Lorient (11.44), Sedan, Neufchateau, Bastogne (12.44), Houffalize (1.45), Lutzkampen, Grosskampenberg, Roseheid (2.45), Gerolstein, Saar-Moselle, Worms, Oppenheim (3.45), Bavaria, Coburg, Rohrbach, Neufelden (4.45), Linz, Austria (5.45)

Notes :

12th ARMORED DIVISION

Activated in the U.S.A. September 1942. Moved overseas September 1944. Returned to the U.S.A. for inactivation December 1945

SHOULDER FLASH

17th Armored Infantry Bn
56th Armored Infantry Bn
66th Armored Infantry Bn

23rd Tank Battalion
43rd Tank Battalion
714th Tank Battalion

493rd Armd Field Artillery Bn
494th Armd Field Artillery Bn
495th Armd Field Artillery Bn

Combat Commands A, B & R

92nd Cavalry Reconnaissance Sqn

119th Armored Engineer Bn

82nd Armored Medical Bn

134th Armored Ordnance Bn

152nd Armored Signals Coy

Insignia as for
1st Armored Divn
except numeral
'12' replaces '1'

UK (10.44), Le Havre (11.44), Weisslingen, Maginot Line, Rohrbach, Utweiler (12.44), Rhine, Herlisheim (1.45), Colmar, Rouffach, St Avoid (2.45), Ludwigshafen, Speyer, Germersheim, Worms, Wurzburg (3.45), Scweinfurt, Dillingen, Lansberg (4.45), Austria (5.45)

Notes :

13th ARMORED DIVISION

Activated in the U.S.A. October 1942. Moved overseas January 1945. Returned to the U.S.A. for inactivation July 1945

16th Armored Infantry Bn
59th Armored Infantry Bn
67th Armored Infantry Bn

93rd Cavalry Reconnaissance Sqn

124th Armored Engineer Bn

24th Tank Battalion
45th Tank Battalion
46th Tank Battalion

83rd Armored Medical Bn

496th Armd Field Artillery Bn
497th Armd Field Artillery Bn
498th Armd Field Artillery Bn

135th Armored Ordnance Bn

153rd Armored Signals Coy

Combat Commands A, B & R

Insignia as for
1st Armored Divn
except numeral
'13' replaces '1'

Le Havre (1.45), Kassel (4.45), Honnef, Siegburg, Bergisch Gladbach, Mettmann, Eschenau, (4.45), Bavaria, Parsberg, Matting, Plattling, (4.45), Austria, Braunau, Marktl.

Notes :

14th ARMORED DIVISION

Activated in the U.S.A. November 1942. Moved overseas October 1944. Returned to the U.S.A. for inactivation September 1945

19th Armored Infantry Bn
62nd Armored Infantry Bn
68th Armored Infantry Bn

94th Cavalry Reconnaissance Sqn

125th Armored Engineer Bn

25th Tank Battalion
47th Tank Battalion
48th Tank Battalion

84th Armored Medical Bn

499th Armd Field Artillery Bn
500th Armd Field Artillery Bn
501st Armd Field Artillery Bn

136th Armored Ordnance Bn

154th Armored Signals Coy

Combat Commands A, B & R

Insignia as for
1st Armored Divn
except numeral
'14' replaces '1'

Marseilles (10.44), Rambervillers, Gerwiller, Benfield, Barr (11.44), Lauter River,
Moder River, Bitche (12.44), Hatten, Rittershoffen (1.45), Moder River, Segfried Line
Germersheim (3.45), Worms, Lohr, Gemunden, Neustadt, Ingolstadt (4.45),Moosburg (5.45)

Notes :

16th ARMORED DIVISION

Activated in the U.S.A. July 1943. Moved overseas February 1945. Returned to the U.S.A. for inactivation October 1945

18th Armored Infantry Bn
64th Armored Infantry Bn
69th Armored Infantry Bn

23rd Cavalry Reconnaissance Sqn

216th Armored Engineer Bn

5th Tank Battalion
16th Tank Battalion
26th Tank Battalion

137th Armored Ordnance Bn

393rd Armd Field Artillery Bn
396rd Armd Field Artillery Bn
397th Armd Field Artillery Bn

216th Armored Medical Bn

156th Armored Signals Coy

Combat Commands A, b & R

Insignia as for
1st Armored Divn
except numeral
'16' replaces '1'

France (2.45), Germany, Nurnberg (4.45), Waidhaus, (5.45), Czechoslovakia, Pilsen (5.45)

Notes :

20th ARMORED DIVISION

Activated in the U.S.A. March 1943. Moved overseas February 1945. Serving with Allied Army of Occupation Southern Germany May 1945

8th Armored Infantry Bn
65th Armored Infantry Bn
70th Armored Infantry Bn

9th Tank Battalion
20th Tank Battalion
27th Tank Battalion

412th Armd Field Artillery Bn
413rd Armd Field Artillery Bn
414th Armd Field Artillery Bn

Combat Commands A, B & R

30th Cavalry Reconnaissance Sqn

220th Armored Engineer Bn

220th Armored Medical Bn

138th Armored Ordnance Bn

160th Armored Signals Coy

Insignia as for
1st Armored Divn
except numeral
'20' replaces '1'

Le Havre (2.45), Buchy (3.45), Germany, Langendernbach, Marktbreit (4.45), Wurzburg, Dorf, Deiningen, River Danube (4.45), Schrobenhausen, Munich (4.45), Wasserburg, Traunstein, Saltzburg (5.45)

Notes :

1st INFANTRY DIVISION

Regular Division in the U.S.A., moved overseas in August 1942. With Allied Army of Occupation, Czeckoslovakia, May 1945

SHOULDER PATCH

16th Infantry Regiment
18th Infantry Regiment
26th Infantry Regiment

5th Field Artillery Bn
7th Field Artillery Bn
32nd Field Artillery Bn
33rd Field Artillery Bn

1st Engineer Battalion

1st Signals Company

701st Ordnance Company

1st Quartermaster Company

1st Reconnaissance Troop

1st Medical Battalion

Red '1' on an
olive-drab
background

Oran (11.42), Tunisia, Maktar, Kasserine (2.43), Mateur (5.43), Sicily (7.43), UK (9.43), Normandy (6.44), Marigny (7.44), Aachen (9.44), Hurtgen Forest (11.44), Ardennes (12.44), Siegfried Line, Roer (2.45), Ramagen (3.45), Ruhr, Paderborn (4.45), Czeckoslovakia, Kinsperk, Sangerberg (5.45)

Notes :

2nd INFANTRY DIVISION

Regular Division in the U.S.A. , moved overseas October 1943. With Allied Army of Occupation, Czeckoslovakia, May 1945

9th Infantry Regiment
23rd Infantry Regiment
38th Infantry Regiment

12th Field Artillery Bn
15th Field Artillery Bn
37th Field Artillery Bn
38th Field Artillery Bn

2nd Engineer Battalion

2nd Signals Company

702nd Ordnance Company

2nd Quartermaster Company

2nd Reconnaissance Troop

2nd Medical Battalion

Indian head on a white star all on a black shield

Red face on indian, white/blue bonnet

UK (10.43), Normandy, Trevieres (6.44), Hill 192 (7.44), Tinchebray (8.44), Brest (9.44), St Vith (10.44), Elsenborn (12.44), St Vith (2.45), Gemund, Breisig, Remagen, Limburg (3.45), Gottingen, Merseburg, Leipzig (4.45), Czeckoslovakia, Pilsen (5.45)

Notes :

3rd INFANTRY DIVISION

Regular Division in the U.S.A., moved overseas October 1942. Located in Austria with Allied Army of Occupation May 1945

7th Infantry Regiment
15th Infantry Regiment
30th Infantry Regiment

9th Field Artillery Bn
10th Field Artillery Bn
39th Field Artillery Bn
41st Field Artillery Bn

10th Engineer Bn

3rd Signals Company

703rd Ordnance Company

3rd Quartermaster Company

3rd Reconnaissance Troop

3rd Medical Battalion

Three white
diagonal bars on
a blue square

French Morocco, Fedala (11.42), Sicily (7.43), Salerno (9.43), Volturno (10.43), Cassino (12.43), Anzio (1.44), Rome (5.44), France, St Tropez (8.44), Strasbourg (11.44), Colmar (1.45), Siegfried Line (3.45), Nurnberg (4.45), Augsburg, Munich, Salzburg (5.45)

Notes :

4th INFANTRY DIVISION

Activated in the U.S.A. June 1940. Moved overseas in January 1944. Serving on Occupation duties May 1945 in Germany

SHOULDER PATCH

8th Infantry Regiment
12th Infantry Regiment
22nd Infantry Regiment

20th Field Artillery Bn
29th Field Artillery Bn
42nd Field Artillery Bn
44th Field Artillery Bn

4th Engineer Bn

4th Signals Company

704th Ordnance Company

4th Quartermaster Company

4th Reconnaissance Troop

4th Medical Battalion

Four green ivy
leaves attached
at the stems and
pointing to four
corners, all on
a brown background

UK (2.44), Normandy, Ste Mere Eglise, Cotentin, Cherbourg (6.44), Periers, Avranches (7.44), Paris (8.44), Belgium, Siegfried Line, Schnee Eifel (9.44), Hurtgen Forest (11.44), Luxembourg, Dickweiler (12.44), Fouhren, Vianden (1.45), Prum (2.45), Kyll, Rhine (3.45), Worms, Wurzburg (3.45), Ochsenfurt (4.45), Miesbach (5.45)

Notes :

5th INFANTRY DIVISION

Activated in the U.S.A. October 1939. Moved overseas April 1942. Located in Czeckoslovakia May 1945

2nd Infantry Regiment
10th Infantry Regiment
11th Infantry Regiment

19th Field Artillery Bn
21st Field Artillery Bn
46th Field Artillery Bn
50th Field Artillery Bn

7th Engineer Bn

5th Signals Company

705th Ordnance Company

5th Quartermaster Company

5th Reconnaissance Troop

5th Medical Battalion

SHOULDER PATCH

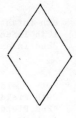

A red Diamond

UK (5.42), Normandy, Caumont, Vidouville (7.44), Angers, Fontainbleau, Reims (8.44), Metz (9.44), Lauterbach (12.44), Ardennes (12.44), Sauer, Siegfried Line (3.45), Rhine, Frankfurt-am Main, Ruhr (4.45), Czeckoslovakia, Volary, Vimpeck (5.45)

Notes :

8th INFANTRY DIVISION

Activated in the U.S.A. July 1940, moved overseas December 1943. Attached to the British 2nd Army, May 1945, Baltic Coast area.

SHOULDER PATCH

13th Infantry Regiment
28th Infantry Regiment
121st Infantry Regiment

8th Signals Company

708th Ordnance Company

28th Field Artillery Bn
43th Field Artillery Bn
45th Field Artillery Bn
56th Field Artillery Bn

8th Quartermaster Company

8th Reconnaissance Troop

12th Engineer Bn

8th Medical Battalion

a gold arrow
piercing a silver
'8' all on a blue
background

UK, Ireland (1.44), Normandy, Ay River (7.44), Rennes (8.44), Brest (9.44), Luxembourg, Hurtgen Forest (11.44), Brandenburg (12.44), Roer River, Duren, Erft Canal (2.45), Rodenkirchen, Koln (3.45), Ruhr Pocket (4.45), Elbe, Schwerin (5.45)

Notes :

9th INFANTRY DIVISION

Activated in the U.S.A. July 1940, moved overseas December 1942. Located in central Germany May 1945

39th Infantry Regiment
47th Infantry Regiment
60th Infantry Regiment

26th Field Artillery Bn
34th Field Artillery Bn
60th Field Artillery Bn
84th Field Artillery Bn

15th Engineer Bn

9th Signals Company

709th Ordnance Company

9th Quartermaster Company

9th Reconnaissance Troop

9th Medical Bn

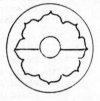

An Octofoil, red over blue with a white centre, all on a khaki disc

North Africa, Algiers, Safi, Port Lyautey (11.42), Spanish Moroccan Border (11.42), Tunisia (2.43), Bizerte (5.43), Sicily (8.43), UK (11.43), Normandy, Cherbourg (6.44), St Lo (7.44), Falaise, Marne (8.44), Saarlautern (8.44), Monschau, Losheim (11.44), Echtz, Schlich (12.44), Remagen (3.45), Ruhr, Nordhausen (4.45), Dessau (5.45)

Notes :

10th MOUNTAIN DIVISION

Formed in the U.S.A. June 1943 as the 10th Light Division (Pack, Alpine) with 87th Mountain Infantry Regiment as a nucleus. Redesignated 10th Mountain Division, moved overseas January 1945. Returned to the U.S.A. for inactivation August 1945

85th Infantry Regiment (2,872)	110th Signals Company (267)
86th Infantry Regiment (2,872)	
87th Infantry Regiment (2,872)	
	710th Ordnance Company (91)
604th Field Artillery Bn)	
605th Field Artillery Bn) (1,738)	10th Quartermaster Bn (459)
616th Field Artillery Bn)	
	10th Reconnaissance Troop (162)
126th Engineer Bn (782)	
10th Anti Tank Bn (347)	10th Medical Battalion (665)

Crossed red bayonets on a blue powder keg edged white. Legend 'MOUNTAIN' above, in white. Fine white outline to the bayonets

Italy, Cutigliano (1.45), Silla, Mount Belvedere (2.45), Canolle (3.45), Mongiorgio, River Po, Pradalbino, Bomporto (4.45), Verona, Torbole (4.45), Lake Garda, Gargnano, Porto de Tremosine (4.45)

Notes : This type of Division totalled 14,101 all ranks and included 6,152 horses and mules, 680 vehicles of all types and 75mm Pack Howitzers (36). The number of personnel in each of the above elements is shown in brackets.

26th INFANTRY DIVISION

Activated in the U.S.A. January 1941, moved overseas August 1944. Located in Czeckoslovakia, May 1945

101st Infantry Regiment
104th Infantry Regiment
328th Infantry Regiment

101st Field Artillery Bn
102nd Field Artillery Bn
180th Field Artillery Bn
263rd Field Artillery Bn

101st Engineer Bn

39th Signals Company

726th Ordnance Company

26th Quartermaster Company

26th Reconnaissance Troop

114th Medical Battalion

Linked letters
'Y' & 'D' in blue
on Khaki diamond
(Yankee Division)

Cherbourg (9.44), Moncourt (10.44), Dieuze (11.44), Saar Union, Maginot Line, Metz (12.44) Luxembourg, Rambrouch, Grosbous, Arsdorf (12.44), Wiltz River, Grumelscheid, Clerf River, Saarlautern (1.45), Merzig, Rhine, Oppenheim, Hanau (3.45), Fulda, Meiningen (4.45), Austria, Linz (4.45), Czeckoslovakia, Vlatava River (4.45)

Notes :

28th INFANTRY DIVISION

Activated in the U.S.A. February 1941, moved overseas October 1943. Returned to the U.S.A. for inactivation August 1945

SHOULDER PATCH

109th Infantry Regiment
110th Infantry Regiment
112th Infantry Regiment

28th Signals Company

728th Ordnance Company

107th Field Artillery Bn
108th Field Artillery Bn
109th Field Artillery Bn
229th Field Artillery Bn

28th Quartermaster Company

28th Reconnaissance Troop

103rd Engineer Bn

103rd Medical Battalion

A red Keystone

UK (11.43), Normandy (7.44), St Lo, Percy, Gathemo, Le Neubourg, Elbeuf, Paris (8.44), Luxembourg, Binsfeld, Siegfried Line (9.44), Elsenborn (10.44), Hurtgen Forest, Schmidt, Vossenack, Luxembourg (11.44), Ardennes, Neuf-Chateau (12.44), Meuse River, Verdun (1.45), Vosges Mountains, Rhine-Rhone Canal (2.45), Julich, Kaiserlautern (4.45)

Notes :

29th INFANTRY DIVISION

Activated in the U.S.A. February 1941, moved overseas October 1942. Returned to the U.S.A. for inactivation January 1946

SHOULDER PATCH

115th Infantry Regiment	29th Signals Company
116th Infantry Regiment	
175th Infantry Regiment	
	729th Ordnance Company
110th Field Artillery Bn	
111th Field Artillery Bn	
224th Field Artillery Bn	29th Quartermaster Company
227th Field Artillery Bn	
	29th Reconnaissance Troop
121st Engineer Bn	
	104th Medical Battalion

Circular disc divided into two parts, left side blue, right side grey

UK (10.42), Normandy, Isigny, Elle River (6.44), St Lo (7.44), Vire, Brest (8.44), Geilenkirchen (10.44), Siersdorf, Setterich, Durboslar, Bettendorf, The Roer (11.44), Julich Sportplatz, Hasenfeld Gut (12.44), The Roer, Julich, Immerath, Munchen-Gladbach (2.45), The Elbe (4.45), Bremen (5.45)

Notes :

30th INFANTRY DIVISION

Activated in the U.S.A. September 1940, moved overseas February 1944. Returned to the U.S.A. August 1945

117th Infantry Regiment	30th Signals Company
119th Infantry Regiment	
120th Infantry Regiment	730th Ordnance Company
113th Field Artillery Bn	
118th Field Artillery Bn	30th Quartermaster Company
197th Field Artillery Bn	
230th Field Artillery Bn	30th Reconnaissance Troop
105th Engineer Bn	
	105th Medical Battalion

Roman numeral 'XXX' with bars and edge in blue on a maroon background

UK (2.44), Normandy, Vire-et-Taute Canal (6.44), Vire River, St Lo (7.44), Mortain (8.44), Belgium, R.Meuse, Liege, Maastricht (9.44), Aachen, Altdorf (10.44), Ardennes, Malmedy (12.44), Lierneux, Aachen (1.45), The Roer, Julich (2.45), The Rhine (3.45), Hamelin, Braunschweig, Magdeburg, Grunewald* (4.45)

Notes :   * Russian Forces contacted

34th INFANTRY DIVISION

A National Guard division from North Dakota, South Dakota, Iowa & Minnesota.
Activated February 1941, moved overseas May 1942, returned to USA November 1945

Red bull's skull
on a mexican jar
in black

133rd Infantry Regiment
135rd Infantry Regiment
168th Infantry Regiment

34th Signals Company

734th Ordnance Company

125th Field Artillery Bn
151th Field Artillery Bn
175th Field Artillery Bn
185th Field Artillery Bn

34th Quartermaster Company

34th Reconnaissance Troop

109th Engineer Bn

109th Medical Battalion

UK (5.42), Algiers (11.42), Fondouk, Tunisia (2.23), Hill 609 (3.43), Tebourba,
Ferryville (5.43), Salerno (9.43), Benevento, The Volturno (10.43), Mt Patano (12.43),
Gustav Line, Mt Trocchio, The Rapido (1.44), Cassino (2.44), Anzio (3.44), Cisterna,
Rome (5.44), Livorno (7.44), Mount Belmont (10.44), Bologna (4,45)

Notes :

35th INFANTRY DIVISION

A National Guard division from Kansas, Missouri and Nebraska. Activated in December 1940, moved overseas may 1944, returned to USA December 1945

SHOULDER PATCH

134th Infantry Regiment 137th Infantry Regiment 320th Infantry Regiment	35th Signals Company
	735th Ordnance Company
127th Field Artillery Bn 161st Field Artillery Bn 216th Field Artillery Bn 219th Field Artillery Bn	35th Quartermaster Company
	35th Reconnaissance Troop
60th Engineer Bn	110th Medical Battalion

A white cross in white wagon wheel on a blue field

UK (5.44), Normandy, Emelie, St Lo (7.44), The Vire, Avranches, Orleans, Sens (8.44), Moselle, Nancy (9.44), Chambrey (10.44), Sarreguemines, Saar River, Blies River (12.44) Belgium, Arlon, Ardennes (12.44), Villers-la-Bonne-Eau, Lutrebois (1.45), Siegfried Line, Roer (2.45), Wesel (3.45), Ruhr, Elbe (4.45), Cobitz, Angern, Hanover (4.45)

Notes :

36th INFANTRY DIVISION

A National Guard division from Texas. Activated in November 1940, moved overseas April 1943. Returned to the U.S.A. in December 1945

SHOULDER PATCH

141st Infantry Regiment
142nd Infantry Regiment
143rd Infantry Regiment

36th Signals Company

736th Ordnance Company

131st Field Artillery Bn
132nd Field Artillery Bn
133rd Field Artillery Bn
155th Field Artillery Bn

36th Quartermaster Company

36th Reconnaissance Troop

111th Engineer Bn

111th Medical Battalion

A blue flint
arrow-head bearing
the letter 'T'
(Texas) in Green

North Africa, Arzew, Rabat (4.43), Salerno (9.43), Agropoli, Altavilla (10.43), Mt Maggiore, Mt Lungo (12.43) Rapido River (1.44), Cassino (2.44), Anzio (5.44), Rome, Magliano, Piombino (6.44), Southern France, Frejus, Rhone, Montelimar (8.44), Moselle (9.44), St Marie Pass (11.44), Colmar (12.44), Mannheim, Wissembourg (2.45)

Notes :

42nd INFANTRY DIVISION

Activated in the U.S.A. July 1943, overseas November 1944. Operated as Task Force Linden to February 1945. Inactivated in Europe June 1946.

222nd Infantry Regiment	42nd Signals Company
232nd Infantry Regiment	
242nd Infantry Regiment	742nd Ordnance Company
232nd Field Artillery Bn	
292nd Field Artillery Bn	42nd Quartermaster Company
402nd Field Artillery Bn	
542nd Field Artillery Bn	42nd Reconnaissance Troop
142nd Engineer Bn	
	122nd Medical Battalion

SHOULDER PATCH

a rainbow, blue lower band, yellow centre band and red outer band

Marseilles (12.44), Strasbourg (12.44), Haguenau (2.45), Siegfried Line, Busenburg, Dahn, The Rhine (3.45), Wertheim, Wurzburg, Schweinfurt, Furth, Donauworth, Dachau, Munich (4.45), Austria, Saltzburg (5.45)

Notes : Task Force Linden comprised the three Infantry Regiments & elements of Divn HQ. The full Division was assembled late January 1945

44th INFANTRY DIVISION

Activated in the U.S.A. September 1940, moved overseas September 1944. Returned to the U.S.A. July 1945

71st Infantry Regiment
114th Infantry Regiment
324th Infantry Regiment

156th Field Artillery Bn
157th Field Artillery Bn
217th Field Artillery Bn
220th Field Artillery Bn

63rd Engineer Bn

44th Signals Company

744th Ordnance Company

44th Quartermaster Company

44th Reconnaissance Troop

119th Medical Battalion

Orange disc with blue border with a pair of black '4's back to back and joined by a common vertical

Cherbourg (9.44), Foret de Parroy, Luneville (10.44), Vosges Mts, Avricourt, Strasbourg (11.44), Ratzwiller, Maginot Line (11.44), Fort Simserhof, Saareguemines (12.44), Worms, Mannheim (3.45), Gross Auheim, Ehingen, Fussen, Berg, Wertach (3.45), Imst, Fern Pass, Inn Valley, Landeck (5.45)

Notes :

45th INFANTRY DIVISION

Activated in the U.S.A. September 1940, moved overseas June 1943. Returned to the U.S.A. September 1945

SHOULDER PATCH

A red diamond
bearing a gold
Thunderbird

157th Infantry Regiment
179th Infantry Regiment
180th Infantry Regiment

45th Signals Company

700th Ordnance Company

158th Field Artillery Bn
160th Field Artillery Bn
171st Field Artillery Bn
189th Field Artillery Bn

45th Quartermaster Company

45th Reconnaissance Troop

120th Engineer Bn

120th Medical Battalion

French Morocco (6.43), Sicily (7.43), Salerno (9.43), Volturno River, Venafro (11.44), St Elia (1.44), Anzio (1.44), The Tiber (6.44), Southern France, St Maxime (8.44), Belfort Gap, Epinal, Vosges Mts, Rambervillers (9.44), Mortagne River (10.44), Maginot Line (11.44), Siegfried Line, Homburg, Rhine (3.45), Nurnberg (4.45), Munich (4.45)

Notes :

63rd INFANTRY DIVISION

Activated in the U.S.A. June 1943, moved overseas November 1944. Returned to the U.S.A. in September 1945

SHOULDER PATCH

253rd Infantry Regiment
254th Infantry Regiment
255th Infantry Regiment

718th Field Artillery Bn
861st Field Artillery Bn
862nd Field Artillery Bn
863rd Field Artillery Bn

263rd Engineer Bn

563rd Signals Company

763rd Ordnance Company

63rd Quartermaster Company

63rd Reconnaissance Troop

363rd Medical Battalion

gold sword with
red tip on a
scarlet flame
all on an olive
drab field

Marseille (11.44) , Rhine (12.44), Willerwald, Saar River (2.45), Gudingen, Siegfried Line, Hassel, Spiesen, Erbach, Neuschloss, Heidelberg (3.45), Mosbach, Adelsheim, Bad Wimpfen, Lampoldshausen (4.45), Weissbach, Leipheim (4.45), Darmstadt, Wursburg (5.45)

Notes : Three Inf Regiments arrived Nov & formed Task Force Harris, which faught as Seventh Army troops on the Rhine. Remainder of Divn arrived Jan 1945, and joined the Task Force in Feb 1945, thereafter operating as 63rd Division.

65th INFANTRY DIVISION

Activated in the U.S.A. August 1943, moved overseas January 1945. Inactivated
August 1945 in Germany

259th Infantry Regiment
260th Infantry Regiment
261st Infantry Regiment

720th Field Artillery Bn
867th Field Artillery Bn
868th Field Artillery Bn
869th Field Artillery Bn

265th Engineer Bn

565th Signals Company

765th Ordnance Company

65th Quartermaster Company

65th Reconnaissance Troop

365th Medical Battalion

SHOULDER PATCH

A white halbard
on a blue shield

Le Havre (1.45), Orsholtz, Wadgassen, Dillingen, Saarlautern, Neunkirchen, Oppenheim,
Rhine (3.45), Langensalza, Struth, Neumarkt, Danube, Regensburg, Passau (4.45), Inn
River, Austria, Linz (5.45)

Notes :

66th INFANTRY DIVISION

Activated in the U.S.A. April 1943, moved overseas December 1944. Returned to the U.S.A. November 1945

black panther's head on orange disc, red border

262nd Infantry Regiment
263rd Infantry Regiment
264th Infantry Regiment

566th Signals Company

766th Ordnance Company

721st Field Artillery Bn
870th Field Artillery Bn
871st Field Artillery Bn
872nd Field Artillery Bn

66th Quartermaster Company

66th Reconnaissance Troop

266th Engineer Bn

366th Medical Battalion

UK (11.44), Cherbourg (12.44)*, Brittany-Loire Area (12.44), St Nazaire, Lorient (2.45), La Croix (4.45)

(The Divn was solely employed in containing the enemy in the St Nazaire/Lorient area)

Notes : * Troopship torpedoed with loss of 750 personnel

69th INFANTRY DIVISION

Activated in the U.S.A. May 1943, moved overseas December 1944. Returned to the U.S.A. in September 1945

SHOULDER PATCH

271st Infantry Regiment
272nd Infantry Regiment
273rd Infantry Regiment

569th Signals Company

769th Ordnance Company

724th Field Artillery Bn
879th Field Artillery Bn
880th Field Artillery Bn
881st Field Artillery Bn

69th Quartermaster Company

69th Reconnaissance Troop

269th Engineer Bn

369th Medical Battalion

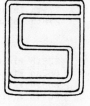

An interlocking red '6' and blue '9' all outlined in white

UK (12.44), Le Havre (1.45), Belgium, Siegfied Line (2.45), Schmidtheim, Dahlem, Rhine, Ehrenbreitstein (3.45), Kassel, Munden, Weissenfels, Leipzig, Eilenburg, Munde River (4.45), Riesa, Torgau (4.45)*

Notes :   * Russian Troops contacted

70th INFANTRY DIVISION

Activated in the U.S.A. June 1943, moved overseas January 1945. Returned to the U.S.A. October 1945

274th Infantry Regiment
275th Infantry Regiment
276th Infantry Regiment

725th Field Artillery Bn
882nd Field Artillery Bn
883rd Field Artillery Bn
884th Field Artillery Bn

270th Engineer Bn

570th Signals Company

770th Ordnance Company

70th Quartermaster Company

70th Reconnaissance Troop

370th Medical Battalion

Red inverted axe head bearing a white axe head and mountain peak and a green fir tree

Bischweiler (12.44), Saarbrucken Area (1.45), Forbach, Stiring-Wendel (2.45), Saarbrucken, Volklingen, Siegfried Line (3.45), Saar Basin (4.45)

Note : The three Infantry Regts arrived Marseilles December 1944 before the other elements of the Division and were formed into Task Force Herren. Placed in the Line at Bischweiler then Saarbrucken, the force joined the other elements of the Division in mid-January 1945

71st INFANTRY DIVISION

Activated in the U.S.A. July 1943, moved overseas January 1945. Returned to the U.S.A. in March 1946 after duty with Army of Occupation

5th Infantry Regiment
14th Infantry Regiment
66th Infantry Regiment

564th Field Artillery Bn
607th Field Artillery Bn
608th Field Artillery Bn
609th Field Artillery Bn

271st Engineer Bn

571st Signals Company

771st Ordnance Company

251st Quartermaster Company

71st Reconnaissance Troop

371st Medical Battalion

White disc with
red border and
numerals '71'
in blue

Le Harve (2.45), Ratswiller, Siegfried Line, Pirmasens, Oppenheim (3.45), Coburg, Bayreuth, Shonfeld, Rosenburg, Kallmunz, Regensburg, Straubing (4.45), Linz (5.45)

Notes : Russian Forces contacted at Linz, 8th May 1945

75th INFANTRY DIVISION

Activated in the U.S.A. in April 1943, moved overseas November 1944. Military Government duties in Westphalia from April 1945

SHOULDER PATCH

289th Infantry Regiment
290th Infantry Regiment
291st Infantry Regiment

575th Signals Company

775th Ordnance Company

730th Field Artillery Bn
897th Field Artillery Bn
898th Field Artillery Bn
899th Field Artillery Bn

75th Quartermaster Company

75th Reconnaissance Troop

275th Engineer Bn

375th Medical Battalion

Square of blue
over red with
white diagonal,
blue '7' and a
red '5', khaki
border

UK (11.44), Le Harve, Yvetot (12.44), Ardennes, Ourthe River (12.44), Grandmenil, Salm River, Vielsalm, Alsace-Lorraine (1.45), Colmar, the Rhine, Luneville (2.45) Holland, Maas River (2.45), Wesel, Homburg, the Rhine (3.45), Haard Forest, Dortmund, Herdecke, Brambauer (4.45)

Notes :

76th INFANTRY DIVISION

Activated in the U.S.A. in June 1942, moved overseas December 1944. Inactivated in Europe, August 1945

304th Infantry Regiment
385th Infantry Regiment
417th Infantry Regiment

302nd Field Artillery Bn
355th Field Artillery Bn
364th Field Artillery Bn
901st Field Artillery Bn

301st Engineer Bn

76th Signals Company

776th Ordnance Company

76th Quartermaster Company

76th Reconnaissance Troop

301st Medical Battalion

Blue over red shield with a khaki divider, white 3-pronged motif

Le Harve, Limesy, Beine, Champlon (1.45), Luxembourg, Echternach, Sauer River, Siegrried Line, Katzenkopf Fortress, Irrel (2.45), Hosten, Speicher, Karl, Moselle, Mulheim, Boppard, Kamberg (3.45), Werra River, Langensalza, Zeitz, Mulde River, Chemnitz (4.45)

Notes :

78th INFANTRY DIVISION

Activated in the U.S.A. in August 1942, moved overseas October 1944. Inactivated May 1946 in Europe following duty with Army of Occupation

309th Infantry Regiment
310th Infantry Regiment
311th Infantry Regiment

307th Field Artillery Bn
308th Field Artillery Bn
309th Field Artillery Bn
903rd Field Artillery Bn

303rd Engineer Bn

78th Signals Company

778th Ordnance Company

78th Quartermaster Company

78th Reconnaissance Troop

303rd Medical Battalion

Red semi-circle
with white lightning

UK (10.44), France, Belgium, Tongres, Germany, Rotgen (11.44), Hurtgen Forest, Simmerath, Witzerath, Bickerath, Kesternich (12.44), Siegfried Line (1.45), Kesternich, Schmidt, Schwammanauel Dam, Roer River (2.45), Remagen, Honnef (3.45), Ruhr Pocket, Marburg (4.45)

Notes :   310th Regiment attached to 9th Armored Division from 1.45

79th INFANTRY DIVISION

Activated in the U.S.A. in June 1942, moved overseas april 1944. Returned to the U.S.A. for inactivation, December 1945

SHOULDER PATCH

313th Infantry Regiment
314th Infantry Regiment
315th Infantry Regiment

310th Field Artillery Bn
311th Field Artillery Bn
312th Field Artillery Bn
904th Field Artillery Bn

304th Engineer Bn

79th Signals Company

779th Ordnance Company

79th Quartermaster Company

79th Reconnaissance Troop

304th Medical Battalion

Blue shield with white border and cross of Lorraine

UK (4.44), Normandy (6.44), Valognes, Fort du Roule, Cherbourg (6.44), La Haye du Puits, Lessay (7.44), Le Mans, the Seine, Therain River (8.44), St Amand, Charmes, Foret de Parroy (9.44), Emberminil, Luneville (10.44), Vesouse & Moder Rivers (11.44), Siegfried Line (12.44), Wissembourg, Maginot Line, Hatten, Rittershoffen, Haguenau (1.45), Rhine, Ruhr Pocket (4.45)

Notes :

80th INFANTRY DIVISION

Activated in the U.S.A. in July 1942, moved overseas July 1944. Returned to the U.S.A. January 1946 for inactivation after serving with Army of Occupation

317th Infantry Regiment
318th Infantry Regiment
319th Infantry Regiment

313rd Field Artillery Bn
314th Field Artillery Bn
315th Field Artillery Bn
905th Field Artillery Bn

305th Engineer Bn

80th Signals Company

780th Ordnance Company

80th Quartermaster Company

80th Reconnaissance Troop

305th Medical Battalion

Gold shield, white borders and three azure blue mountain peaks

(Blue Ridge Mts)

Normandy (8.44), Evron, St Suzanne, Argentan, Falaise (8.44), St Mihiel, Chalons, Commercy, Seille River (9.44), Delme Ridge, St Avold (11.44), Zweibrucken, Luxembourg, Bastogne (12.44), Dahl, Goesdorf, Wiltz River (1.45), Wallendorf, Siegfried Line (2.45), Kaiserlautern, Mainz (3.45), Erfurt, Weimar, Nurnburg (4.45), Regensburg, R.Enns (5.45)

Notes :

83rd INFANTRY DIVISION

Activated in the U.S.A. in August 1942, moved overseas April 1944. Returned to the U.S.A. for inactivation April 1946 after service with Army of Occupation.

329th Infantry Regiment	83rd Signals Company
330th Infantry Regiment	
331st Infantry Regiment	783rd Ordnance Company
322nd Field Artillery Bn	
323rd Field Artillery Bn	83rd Quartermaster Company
324th Field Artillery Bn	
908th Field Artillery Bn	
	83rd Reconnaissance Troop
308th Engineer Bn	
	308th Medical Battalion

UK (4.44), Normandy, Carantan (6.44), St Lo (7.44), Dinard, St Malo, St Servan, Rennes (8.44), Ile de Cezembre, Luxembourg, Remich (9.44), Echternach (10.44), Hurtgen Forest, the Roer (11.44), Rochefort (12.44), Belgium, Holland (1.45), the Rhine, Wesel, Bodenwerder (3.45), Halle, Harz Mts, Barby (4.45)

Notes : withdrew from the Elbe at Barby, April 1945 to allow Russian Occupation

SHOULDER PATCH

Black inverted triangle, gold circle and the monogram O H I O contained within

84th INFANTRY DIVISION

Activated in the U.S.A. in October 1942. Moved overseas September 1944. Returned to the U.S.A. for inactivation, January 1946 after service with Army of Occupation

333rd Infantry Regiment
334th Infantry Regiment
335th Infantry Regiment

325th Field Artillery Bn
326th Field Artillery Bn
327th Field Artillery Bn
909th Field Artillery Bn

309th Engineer Bn

84th Signals Company

784th Ordnance Company

84th Quartermaster Company

84th Reconnaissance Troop

309th Medical Battalion

A white axe splitting a rail on a red disc

UK (10.44), Normandy, Holland, Gulpen (11.44), Geilenkirchen, Beeck, Lindern (11.44), Wurm, Mulendorf (12.44), Belgium, Verdenne (12.44), Beffe, Laroche (1.45), Roer River, Boisheim (2.45), Dulken, Krefeld, Rhine (3.45), Lembeck, Hanover (4.45), Balow (5.45)

Notes : Russian Forces contacted at Balow, May 1945

85th INFANTRY DIVISION

Activated in the U.S.A. in May 1942, moved overseas December 1943. Returned to the U.S.A. August 1945

SHOULDER PATCH

337th Infantry Regiment
338th Infantry Regiment
339th Infantry Regiment

85th Signals Company

328th Field Artillery Bn
329th Field Artillery Bn
403rd Field Artillery Bn
910th Field Artillery Bn

785th Ordnance Company

85th Quartermaster Company

310th Engineer Bn

85th Reconnaissance Troop

310th Medical Battalion

A khaki disc bearing the letters 'C' and 'D' in red

(Custer Division)

Morocco, Casablanca (1.44), Algeria, Oran (2.44), Naples (3.44), Gustav Line (4.44), Solacciano, Castellonorato, Formia, Itri, Terracina, Sezze, Lariano (5.44), Rome (6.44), Arno River (8.44), Gothic Line, Firenzuola (9.44), La Martina, Mt Mezzano, Pizzano, (10.45), Gothic Line (1.45), Lucca, Po Valley, Panaro River (4.45)

Notes :

86th INFANTRY DIVISION

Activated in the U.S.A. in December 1942, moved overseas February 1945. Returned to the U.S.A. in June 1945. Left San Francisco for the Philippines, August 1945

341st Infantry Regiment	86th Signals Company
342nd Infantry Regiment	
343rd Infantry Regiment	786th Ordnance Company
331st Field Artillery Bn	
332nd Field Artillery Bn	86th Quartermaster Company
404th Field Artillery Bn	
911th Field Artillery Bn	
	86th Reconnaissance Troop
311th Engineer Bn	
	311th Medical Battalion

Red shield with a black hawk, the hawk bearing a red shield with letters 'B' & 'H' in black

(Black Hawk Divn)

France (3.45), Germany, Koln, Weiden (3.45), Eibelshausen, Attendorn, the Ruhr, Ansbach, Eichstatt, Danube, Mittel Isar Canal (4.45), Waserburg, Saltzburg (5.45)

Notes :

87th INFANTRY DIVISION

Activated in the U.S.A. in December 1942, moved overseas October 1944. Returned to the U.S.A. July 1945

345th Infantry Regiment
346th Infantry Regiment
347th Infantry Regiment

334th Field Artillery Bn
335th Field Artillery Bn
336th Field Artillery Bn
912th Field Artillery Bn

312th Engineer Bn

87th Signals Company

787th Ordnance Company

87th Quartermaster Company

87th Reconnaissance Troop

312th Medical Battalion

A golden acorn
on a green disc

UK (10.44), France, Metz, Fort Driant, Rimling, Guiderkirch (12.44), Belgium, Ramagen, (12.44), Germont, Ourthe (1.45), Luxembourg, Wasserbillig, Schlierbach, Hogden (1.45), Neuendorf, Hallschlag (2.45), Dollendorf, Koblenz, Rhine, Langgons (3.45), Thuringia, Saxony, Plauen (4.45), Falkenstein (5.45)

Notes :

88th INFANTRY DIVISION

Activated in the U.S.A. in July 1942, moved overseas December 1943. With Allied Army of Occupation, June 1945

349th Infantry Regiment
350th Infantry Regiment
351st Infantry Regiment

88th Signals Company

788th Ordnance Company

337th Field Artillery Bn
338th Field Artillery Bn
339th Field Artillery Bn
913th Field Artillery Bn

88th Quartermaster Company

88th Reconnaissance Troop

313th Engineer Bn

313th Medical Battalion

Infantry blue quatre-foil in form of two '8's crossed

Morocco, Casablanca (12.43), Algeria, Magenta (12.43), Naples, Cassino (2.44), Garagliano River, Minturno (3.44), Spigno, Itri, Roccagorga, Anzio (5.44), Rome (6.44) Pomerance, Volterra, Arno (7.44), Gothic Line, Mt Battaglia (9.44), Farnetto (10.44), Loiano-Livergnano (1.45), Po River, Verona, Brenta River (4.45), Dolomites (5.45)

Notes :

89th INFANTRY DIVISION

Activated in the U.S.A. in July 1942, moved overseas January 1945. Returned to the U.S.A. in December 1945

353rd Infantry Regiment
354th Infantry Regiment
355th Infantry Regiment

89th Signals Company

789th Ordnance Company

340th Field Artillery Bn
341st Field Artillery Bn
563rd Field Artillery Bn
914th Field Artillery Bn

405th Quartermaster Company

89th Reconnaissance Troop

314th Engineer Bn

314th Medical Battalion

Khaki disc with
a black 'W' in
a black circle

(Middle-West)

France, Le Havre (1.45), Echternach, the Sauer, the Moselle, the Rhine (3.45), Friedrichroda, Zwickau (4.45)

Notes :

90th INFANTRY DIVISION

Activated in the U.S.A. in March 1942, moved overseas March 1944. Returned to the U.S.A. in December 1945

357th Infantry Regiment
358th Infantry Regiment
359th Infantry Regiment

343rd Field Artillery Bn
344th Field Artillery Bn
345th Field Artillery Bn
915th Field Artillery Bn

315th Engineer Bn

90th Signals Company

790th Ordnance Company

90th Quartermaster Company

90th Reconnaissance Troop

315th Medical Battalion

SHOULDER PATCH

Red 'T' bisecting a red 'O' on a khaki square

(Texas-Oklahoma)

UK (4.44), Normandy, Pont l'Abbe (6.44), Foret de Mont Castre, Seves, Periers (7.44), Sarthe River, Falaise, Chambois (8.44), Verdun, Metz (9.44), Moselle (11.44), Saarlautern (12.44), Ardennes, Oberhausen (1.45), Siegfried Line, Prum River (2.45), Mainz, the Rhine, the Main, the Werra (3.45), Sudeten hills (4.45)

Notes :

91st INFANTRY DIVISION

Activated in the U.S.A. in August 1942, moved overseas April 1944. Returned to the U.S.A. in September 1945

361st Infantry Regiment
362nd Infantry Regiment
363rd Infantry Regiment

346th Field Artillery Bn
347th Field Artillery Bn
348th Field Artillery Bn
916th Field Artillery Bn

316th Engineer Bn

91st Signals Company

791st Ordnance Company

91st Quartermaster Company

91st Reconnaissance Troop

316th Medical Battalion

Green Fir tree
(Powder River)

Morocco, Arzew, Renan (4.44), Italy, Chianni, Liverno (7.44), Arno River (8.44), Gothic Line, Monticelli, Santerno River (9.44), Livergnano, Pianoro (10.44), Bologna, Po River, Adige River, Treviso (4.45), Venezia-Giulia (5.45)

Notes : 361st RCT landed Anzio and fought at Velletri, 363rd RCT entered combat near Riparbella. The complete Division entered combat July 1944

92nd INFANTRY DIVISION

Activated in the U.S.A. in October 1942, moved overseas September 1944. Returned to the U.S.A. in November 1945

365th Infantry Regiment
370th Infantry Regiment
371st Infantry Regiment

92nd Signals Company

792nd Ordnance Company

597th Field Artillery Bn
598th Field Artillery Bn
599th Field Artillery Bn
600th Field Artillery Bn

92nd Quartermaster Company

92nd Reconnaissance Troop

317th Engineer Bn

317th Medical Battalion

Black Buffalo on olive drab, black border

Naples (10.44)*, Serchio River, Castelnuovo (11.44), Ligurian Coast (4.45)

Notes :   370th RCT arrived 8.44, attached 1st Armored Divn. Operated on Ligurian Coast sector as Task Force 92 until joined by the Division.

94th INFANTRY DIVISION

Activated in the U.S.A. in September 1942, moved overseas August 1944. Returned to U.S.A. February 1946

301st Infantry Regiment
302nd Infantry Regiment
376th Infantry Regiment

94th Signals Company

794th Ordnance Company

301st Field Artillery Bn
356th Field Artillery Bn
390th Field Artillery Bn
919th Field Artillery Bn

94th Quartermaster Company

94th Reconnaissance Troop

319th Engineer Bn

319th Medical Battalion

A disc divided diagonally into grey & black. Black '9' and Grey '4'

UK (9.44), Normandy (9.44), Lorient, St Nazaire (9.44), Saar-Moselle (1.45), Tettingen, Butzdorf, Nennig, Berg, Wies, Orscholz (1.45), Campholz Woods, Sinz, Munzigen Ridge, Saar (2.45), Zerf, Lampaden, Ollmuth, The Rhine, Ludwigshaven (3.45), Krefeld (4.45), Dusseldorf (5.45)

Notes :

95th INFANTRY DIVISION

Activated in the U.S.A. in July 1942, moved overseas August 1944. Returned to the U.S.A. June 1945

377th Infantry Regiment
378th Infantry Regiment
379th Infantry Regiment

358th Field Artillery Bn
359th Field Artillery Bn
360th Field Artillery Bn
920th Field Artillery Bn

320th Engineer Bn

95th Signals Company

795th Ordnance Company

95th Quartermaster Company

95th Reconnaissance Troop

320th Medical Battalion

Red '9' and
white 'V' on
blue background

UK (8.44), France, Norroy-le-Sec (9.44), Moselle, Cheminot (10.44), Maizieres, Bertrange, Metz, Saar (11.44), Saarlautern (12.44), Holland, Maastricht (2.45), Meerselo (2.45), Julich, Uerdingen, Neuss (2.45), Beckum, Lippe River, Hamm, Kamen, Ruhr & Mohne Rivers, Dortmund (3.45)

Notes :

97th INFANTRY DIVISION

Activated in the U.S.A. in February 1943, moved overseas February 1945 for Europe. Left Europe June 1945 for redeployment at Cebu, Philippine Islands.

303rd Infantry Regiment
386th Infantry Regiment
387th Infantry Regiment

303rd Field Artillery Bn
365th Field Artillery Bn
389th Field Artillery Bn
922nd Field Artillery Bn

322nd Engineer Bn

97th Signals Company

797th Ordnance Company

97th Quartermaster Company

97th Reconnaissance Troop

322nd Medical Battalion

White trident,
blue background

France, Le Havre (3.45), The Rhine (3.45), Bonn, Sieg River, Siegburg, Solingen, Dusseldorf (3.45), Czechoslovakia, Cheb, Widen (4.45), Konstantinovy Lazne (5.45), Le Havre (6.45)

Notes :

99th INFANTRY DIVISION

Activated in the U.S.A. in November 1942, moved overseas September 1944. Returned to U.S.A. September 1945.

393rd Infantry Regiment
394th Infantry Regiment
395th Infantry Regiment

99th Signals Company

799th Ordnance Company

370th Field Artillery Bn
371st Field Artillery Bn
372nd Field Artillery Bn
924th Field Artillery Bn

99th Quartermaster Company

99th Reconnaissance Troop

324th Engineer Bn

324th Medical Battalion

Black shield, white and blue squares

UK (10.44), France, Le Havre (11.44), Belgium, Aubel (11.44), Roer River, Siegfried Line, Elsenborn (12.44), Monchau Forest (2.45), Erft Canal, Remagen, Linz, Giessen (3.45), Schwarzenau, Iserlohn, Altmuhl River, The Danube (4.45), Inn River (5.45), Giesenhausen (5.45)

Notes :

100th INFANTRY DIVISION

Activated in the U.S.A. in November 1942, moved overseas October 1944. With Army of Occupation September 1945

397th Infantry Regiment
398th Infantry Regiment
399th Infantry Regiment

373rd Field Artillery Bn
374th Field Artillery Bn
375th Field Artillery Bn
925th Field Artillery Bn

325th Engineer Bn

100th Signals Company

800th Ordnance Company

100th Quartermaster Company

100th Reconnaissance Troop

325th Medical Battalion

Blue shield, numeral '100' upper half in white, lower half in gold

France, Marseeilles (10.44), Vosges Mountains, Remy, Baccarat, Bertrichamps, St Blaise (11.44), Bitche, Wingen, Lemberg, Reyersweiler, Fort Schiesseck (12.44), Bitche, Neustadt, Ludwigshaven, The Rhine (3.45), Neckar River, Heilbron, Stuttgart (4.45), Goppingen (5.45)

Notes

102nd INFANTRY DIVISION

Activated in the U.S.A. in September 1942, moved overseas September 1944. Returned to U.S.A. March 1946

405th Infantry Regiment
406th Infantry Regiment
407th Infantry Regiment

379th Field Artillery Bn
380th Field Artillery Bn
381st Field Artillery Bn
927th Field Artillery Bn

327th Engineer Bn

102nd Signals Company

802nd Ordnance Company

102nd Quartermaster Company

102nd Reconnaissance Troop

327th Medical Battalion

Golden 'O' & 'Z' on a blue background

(Ozark Divn)

France, Cherbourg (9.44), Netherlands (10.44), Wurm River, Welz, Flossdorf, Linnich (11.44), Roer River (12.44), Lovenich, Krefeld, Homburg-Dusseldorf (2.45), The Rhine, Wilsede, Hessisch-Oldendorf, The Elbe, Breitenfeld (4.45), Gotha (5.45)

Notes :

103rd INFANTRY DIVISION

Activated in the U.S.A. in November 1942, moved overseas October 1944. Returned to U.S.A. September 1945

SHOULDER PATCH

409th Infantry Regiment
410th Infantry Regiment
411th Infantry Regiment

103rd Signals Company

803rd Ordnance Company

382nd Field Artillery Bn
383rd Field Artillery Bn
384th Field Artillery Bn
928th Field Artillery Bn

103rd Quartermaster Company

103rd Reconnaissance Troop

328th Engineer Bn

328th Medical Battalion

Yellow disc,
green cactus,
blue ground

France, Marseilles (10.44), Chevry, St Die, Diefenbach (11.44), Selestat, Griesbach, Lauter River, Sarreguemines (12.44), Sauer River, Moder (1.45), Muhlhausen, Lauter River, Rhine Valley (3.45), Stuttgart, Munsinger, Ulm (4.45), Brenner Pass, Insbruck, (5.45)

Notes :

104th INFANTRY DIVISION

Activated in the U.S.A. in September 1942, moved overseas August 1944. Returned to U.S.A. July 1945

413rd Infantry Regiment
414th Infantry Regiment
415th Infantry Regiment

104th Signals Company

804th Ordnance Company

385th Field Artillery Bn
386th Field Artillery Bn
387th Field Artillery Bn
929th Field Artillery Bn

104th Quartermaster Company

104th Reconnaissance Troop

329th Engineer Bn

329th Medical Battalion

Grey Timberwolf's
head on balsam
green disc

France (9.44), Belgium, Wuestwezel, Zundert, Leur, Etten (10.44), Zevenbergen, Aachen, Stolberg, Eschweiler, Inden (11.44), Lucherberg, Duren, Merken (12.44), North Duren, Birkesdorf (2.45), Koln, Honnef (3.45), Medebach, Paderborn, River Weser, Halle, Mulde River, Pretzsch (4.45)

Notes :   Red Army contacted at Pretzsch, April 1945

106th INFANTRY DIVISION

Activated in the U.S.A. in March 1943, moved overseas November 1944. Returned to the U.S.A. October 1945

422nd Infantry Regiment
423rd Infantry Regiment
424th Infantry Regiment

589th Field Artillery Bn
590th Field Artillery Bn
591st Field Artillery Bn
592nd Field Artillery Bn

81st Engineer Bn

106th Signals Company

806th Ordnance Company

106th Quartermaster Company

106th Reconnaissance Troop

331st Medical Battalion

Blue disc,
golden lions
head, white inner
& red outer border

UK (11.44), France (12.44), Schnee Eifel, Schonberg*, Vielsalm (12.44), Belgium, Anthisnes (1.44), Ennal-Logbierme, Stavelot (1.44), Olds, St Quentin**(3.44)

Notes : * Lost the 422nd & 423rd Inf Regts to the Germans, 424th Attached 7 Armored Divn

** For rehabilitation & reconstruction. Remainder of time in Europe delegated to POW and Occupation duties.

MAIN U.S. GUN TANKS - TYPICAL MODELS

DESIGNATION	M3 Light Tank (Stuart)	M3 Med Tank (Lee)	M4 Med Tank (Sherman)	M4A3E8 Med Tank (Sherman)	M24 Light Tank (Chaffee)	M26 Heavy Tank (Pershing)
MAIN ARMAMENT	1 x 37mm Gun	1 x 37mm Gun 1 x 75mm Gun	1 x 75mm Gun	1 x 76mm Gun	1 x 75mm Gun	1 x 90mm Gun
ROUNDS STOWED	103(M3),116(/A1) 174(/A3)	178 x 37mm 46 x 75mm	97 x 75mm	71 x 76mm	48 x 75mm	70 x 90mm
SECONDARY ARMAMENT	3 x .3MG (/A1)	3-4 x .3MG	2 x .3MG 1 x .5MG	2 x .3MG 1 x .5MG	2 x .3MG 1 x .5MG	2 x .3MG 1 x .5MG
ROUNDS STOWED	6400-8270	9200	4750 & 500	6250 & 600	3750	5000 & 550
WEIGHT	12-14 tons	27 tons	29 tons	32 tons	18 tons	41 tons
SPEED	36(20) mph	26(16) mph	26(18) mph	30(20) mph	35(25) mph	20(5) mph
ROAD RANGE	100 miles	120 miles	120 miles	90 miles	100 miles	90 miles
ENGINE	Contl.W670	Contl.R975	Contl.R975	Ford GAA-III.V8	Cad Twin 44T24	Ford GAF V8
ARMOUR						
Hull Nose	51mm	50mm	51mm	64mm	25mm	76mm
Glacis	13mm	50mm	51mm	64mm	25mm	102mm
Drivers Plate	38mm	50mm	-	-	-	-
Hull Sides	25mm	38mm	38mm	38mm	19-25mm	51-76mm
Decking	10mm	13mm	19mm	19mm	13mm	7-8mm
Belly	10-12mm	13-25mm	13-25mm	25mm	9-13mm	13-25mm
Turret Front	38mm	50mm	76mm	64mm	38mm	102mm
Turret Sides	30mm	50mm	51mm	64mm	25mm	76mm
Turret Top	13mm	25mm	25mm	25mm	13mm	51mm
VERTICAL STEP	2ft 0in	2ft 0in	2ft 0in	2ft 0in	3ft 0in	3ft 10in
TRENCH CROSSING	6ft 0in	7ft 6in	7ft 6in	7ft 6in	8ft 0in	8ft 6in
WADING	3ft 0in	3ft 4in	3ft 0in	3ft 0in	3ft 4in	4ft 0in

ARMOURED VEHICLES & SELF-PROPELLED ARTILLERY

DESIGNATION	M7 GMC	M8 HMC	M10 GMC	M12 GMC	M18 Hellcat	M36 GMC
SERVICE	1942	1942	1943	1943	1943	1944
CHASSIS	M3 Med Tank	M5 Light Tank	M4A2 Med Tank	M3 Med Tank	Special	M10A1 GMC
MAIN ARMAMENT	105mm Howz	75mm Howz	3in Gun	155mm Gun	76mm Gun	90mm Gun
ROUNDS STOWED	69 x 105mm	46 x 75mm	54 x 3in	10 x 155mm	45 x 76mm	47 x 90mm
SECONDARY ARMAMENT	1 x .5MG	2 x .3MG	1 x .5MG	nil	1 x .5MG	1 x .5MG
WEIGHT	23 tons	16 tons	29 tons	26 tons	18 tons	28 tons
SPEED	25(15) mph	36(24) mph	30(20) mph	24(12) mph	45(20) mph	30(18) mph
RANGE	85 miles	100 miles	200 miles	140 miles	150 miles	150 miles

DESIGNATION	M4/M21 MMC	M5 Tractor 13t	M8 Greyhound	M30 Gun Limber	M3 GMC, T19 HMC	M16 MGMC
SERVICE	1942	1942	1943	1943	1943	1943
CHASSIS	Half-Track	M3 Light Tank	A/Car 6 x 6	M3 Med Tank	Half-Track	Half-Track
ARMAMENT	81mm Mortar 1 x .5MG	105mm, 155mm & 4.5in (Towed)	1 x 37mm Gun 1 x .5 MG 1 x .3 MG	1 x .5MG, used with M12 GMC one per gun	75mm M3 GMC 105mm T19 HMC	4 x .5MG in Maxson turret
ROUNDS STOWED	96 x 81mm	24 x 155mm 56 x 105mm	80 x 37mm	40 x 155mm	59 x 75mm 8 x 105mm	5000 x .5MG
WEIGHT	9 tons	13 tons	7 tons	21 tons	9 tons	9 tons
SPEED	45 mph max	35 mph max	55 mph max	24(12) mph	45 mph max	45 mph max
RANGE	210 miles	125 miles	350 miles	140 miles	210 miles	210 miles

HMC = Howitzer Motor Carriage   GMC = Gun Motor Carriage   MGMG = Multiple Gun Motor Carriage
MMC = Mortar Motor Carriage   A/Car = Armoured Car   Half-Track = M2 or M3 series (based on)

GUN PERFORMANCE

TYPE/DESIGNATION	RATE/RANGE	PROJECTILE	GUN WEIGHT
Automatic Rifle, Browning, .3 cal, M1919A2	500-600 rds/min (box feed 20)	.3 cal bullet	19 lbs
Machine Gun, water cooled, .3 cal, M1917A1	450-600 rds/min (belt feed 250)	.3 cal bullet	87 lbs
Machine Gun, air cooled, .3 cal, M1919	450-500 rds/min (belt feed 250)	.3 cal bullet	31 lbs
Machine Gun, Browning, .5 cal, M2	450-575 rds/min (belt feed 110)	.5 cal bullet	84 lbs
Mortar, 60mm, M2	100-1985 yds (1.1 miles)	3 lb HE	42 lbs
Mortar, 81mm, M1	100-3920 yds (2.2 miles)	7 & 10 lb HE	136 lbs
Mortar, 4.2in	100-5000 yds (2.9 miles)	HE/chem/smoke	-
Howitzer, Light Pack, 75mm, M1A1	9760 yds (5.5 miles)	14 lb shell	0.9 tons
Howitzer, Field, 105mm, M2A1	12,500 yds (7.1 miles)	33 lb shell	1.9 tons
Gun, Medium, 4.5in, M1	25,715 yds (14.6 miles)	55 lb shell	5.6 tons
Howitzer, Medium, 155mm, M1918	12,300 yds (7 miles)	95 lb shell	3.7 tons
Howitzer, Medium, 155mm, M1918 (improved)	16,000 yds (9.1 miles)	95 lb shell	5.3 tons
Gun, Heavy, 155mm, M1 & M1A1	20,100 yds (11.4 miles)	95 lb shell	11.4 tons
Gun, Heavy, 8in, M1	35,000 yds (19.9 miles)	240 lb shell	30.9 tons
Howitzer, Heavy, 8in, M1	18,510 yds (10.5 miles)	200 lb shell	13.3 tons
Howitzer, Heavy, 240mm, M1	25,168 yds (14.3 miles)	360 lb shell	28.9 tons
Gun, Quadruple, AA, .5 cal (Maxson Turret)	2300 rds/min	.5 cal bullet	1.1 tons
Gun, AA, 37mm, M1	120 rds/min to 10,500ft	1 lb shell	2.7 tons
Gun, AA, 40mm, Bofors	120 rds/min to 11,000ft	2 lb shell	2.5 tons
Gun, AA, 3in, M3	25 rds/min to 27,900ft	13 lb shell	7.5 tons
Gun, AA, 90mm, M1	15 rds/min to 33,800ft	23 lb shell	8.5 tons
Gun, AA, 90mm, M2	27 rds/min to 33,800ft	23 lb shell	14.4 tons
Gun, Anti-Tank, 37mm, M3A1	2.1in armor at 1000 yds	2 lb shell	0.4 tons
Gun, Anti-Tank, 57mm, M1	2.7in armor at 1000 yds	6 lb shell	1.2 tons
Gun, Anti-Tank, 3in, M1	3.8in armor at 1000 yds	13 lb shell	2.6 tons
Projector, Anti-Tank, bazooka, M1 & M9	4.7in armor at 10 yds	3 lb rocket	-
Tank Gun, 75mm, M3	2.8in armor at 500 yds	AP shot	(see
Tank Gun, 76mm, M1	5.3in armor at 1000 yds	HVAP shot	vehicles)
Tank Gun, 90mm, M3	7.7in armor at 1000 yds	HVAP shot	

VEHICLE COLOURS - SUMMARY (SPECS FM-5-20/21 1942, FM-5-20B 1943, TM-5-267 1943)

Colours Available				Use by Theatre				
No 1	Light Green	34151/30E8 *1		1942	N.Africa *2		Olive Drab	34087/4F4
No 2	Dark Green	34102/30F5					Black	37038
No 3	Sand	30277/5C3		1943	N.Africa		Sand	30277/5C3
No 4	Field Drab	30118/5E4					Earth Yellow	30257/5D7
No 5	Earth Brown	30099/6F5					Black	37038
No 6	Earth Yellow	30257/5D7		1943	Sicily		Olive Drab	34087/4F4
No 7	Loam	34086/5F3				or	Earth Yellow	30257/5D7
No 8	Earth Red	30117/7E6					Earth Red	30117/7E6
No 9	Olive Drab	34087/4F4		1943	Italy		Black	37038
No 10	Black	37038				or	Earth Red	30117/7E6
No 11	Forest Green	34079/30F4				or	Field Drab	30118/5E4
No 12	Desert Sand	30279/7C4					Earth Brown	30099/6F5
							White *3	not Known
							Olive Drab	34087/4F4
				1944	Italy		Olive Drab	34087/4F4
						or	Sand	30277/5C3
							Earth Red	30117/7E6
				1944	N.Europe		Olive Drab	34087/4F4
						or	Black	37038
							Earth Brown	30099/6F5

*1 The Standard numbers in the Right-hand
    column represent the Federal Standard
    Code and the Methuen equivalent

Notes :   *2   Many vehicles had been shipped to N.Africa before Std FM-5-20 was available. These were painted
               Olive Drab overall to which a disruptive pattern was added from local mud roughly applied.

          *3   The use of white was intended to disrupt areas of deep shadow on the vehicle, not widely used.
               The basic vehicle colour was normally Olive Drab with other colours as a disruptive pattern.
               Winter white was applied roughly by mop or brush from a mixture of lime and salt.
               The application of camouflage was the responsibility of the U.S. Corps of Engineers.

NATIONAL IDENTIFICATION SYMBOL ('ALLIED' WHITE STAR MARKINGS)

Numerals below represent star dia in inches. Items marked thus * are included in 1945 regulations only. Other items from 1942 regulations. Star predominantly white (some yellow)	CARS	JEEPS	COMMAND CARS	CARRIER-WPNS ½ton	CARRIER-WPNS ¼ton	TRUCK-CARGO 1½tons	TRUCK-CARGO 2½tons	TRUCK-CARGO 4tons	SCOUT CARS	HALF-TRACKS	Air recognition stars have a circum-circle to distinguish from German cross. Broad circle used on vehicles in Sicily.	LIGHT TANKS	MEDIUM TANKS	M8 ARMORED CAR*	105mm M7 GMC*	M3 MEDIUM TANK*	M4 MEDIUM TANK*	TANK DESTROYERS*
F.Bumper - center	4	4	4	4	6	6	6	6	.	.	Turret rear	.	20	.	.	.	.	.
Radiator - center	.	.	.	.	.	.	.	.	20	20	Turret sides	20	20	16	.	.	.	.
Rear side doors	20	.	.	.	.	.	.	.	.	.	Turret top	20	20	.	.	20	20	.
Center of sides	.	.	.	.	10	.	.	.	20	20	Hull sides	16*	.	.	20	.	.	20
Cab doors	.	.	.	.	.	25	25	25	.	.	Hull sides aft	.	.	16	.	.	.	.
Sides - open cab	.	.	.	.	.	15	15	.	.	.	Hull rear	.	.	16	.	.	.	20
Rear of vehicle	15	.	.	.	.	.	.	.	.	.	Hull rear center	10	.	.	.	16	.	.
Left of rear	.	12	.	.	.	.	.	.	.	.	Hull rear left	.	.	.	16	.	.	.
Center of rear	.	.	10	10	.	10	10	10	15	15	Hull rear right	.	.	.	16	.	.	.
Roof top	36*	.	.	.	.	36	32	32	.	.	Hull front	.	.	16	.	.	.	.
Bonnet top	.	15	15	20	25*	25	32	25	36	36	Hull front center	.	.	.	.	25	.	.
Left R. mudguard	.	.	.	.	.	16	16	15	.	.	Glacis	.	.	.	25	.	25	.
Rear of sides	.	6	15	10	.	.	.	.	.	.	Engine deck top	.	36	36	.	36	60	45

Notes : a) Single point of star at top (vertical surfaces) and rear (horizontal surfaces)
b) Use of Stars & Stripes National insignia confined to N.Africa, deleted from markings by 1943
c) When star colour blended with vehicle colour, a blue disc was used with star superimposed

VEHICLE UNIT IDENTIFICATION ('BUMPER CODES')

COMMAND UNITS (a)	REGIMENT OR BATTALION (c)	COMPANY, BATTERY OR SQUADRON (d)	EXAMPLES (f)

ARMY : Comprised the Army number in Arabic numerals followed by the letter 'A'
 	
eg 5A = US 5th ARMY
 	
CORPS: Comprised the Corps number in Roman numerals followed by AB (Airborne) or (Armored). Numeral only for Infantry
 	
eg IV = 4 Corps (Inf)
I△ = 1 Armd Corps
 	
DIVISIONS (b)
 	
DIVN : Comprised Division number in Arabic numerals followed by AB (Airborne) or (Armored). Numeral only for Infantry (see also col f)
	The Regiment/Battalion number comprised the numerals in Arabic together with the Arm-of Service code as appropriate. A selection of codes aplicable to Regiments/Battalions under Divisional command is listed below :-
	
	AB Airborne
	△ Armored
	F
	FA Field Artillery
	E Engineer
	-I Infantry
	M Medical
	AA Anti-Aircraft (Airborne)
	MN* Mountain
	X Used by indpdt Coys reporting directly to a higher formation
		A letter code was used to identify units of Company size. This could take the form of the Coy letter (A, B,C,D,HQ) or by Arm of Service codes as follows :
		
		AM* Ammunition
		AT Anti Tank
		SV Service
		HW Heavy Wpns
		MT Maintenance
		-O Ordnance
		MR* Mortar
		R Recce
		RT* Rocket
		S Signals
		Q Quartermaster
		
		PLATOON OR TROOP (e)
		
		Vehicle no within the unit eg
		HQ Pln 1-10
		1st Pln 11-20
		2nd Pln 21-30 etc
			`13AB 153AA` `B6`
			
			13th Airborne Division, 153rd AA Bn, B Bty, 6th vehicle
			
			`7△  X` `HQ26`
			
			7th Armored Division, Headquarters Coy, 26th vehicle
			
			`2   5F` `C7`
			
			2nd Infantry Division, 5th Field Arty Bn, C Bty, 7th vehicle
			
			`1△  14-I` `A10`
			
			1st Armored Division, 14th Armd Inf Bn, A Coy, 10th vehicle
			
			`104  X` `R10`
			
			104th Infantry Division, Recce Troop, 10th vehicle

items thus * from 1945 regulations, all other items 1942 regulations

1st ARMORED DIVISION (N.AFRICA 1942)

		HQ Coy	A,D,G Coys	B,E,H Coys	C,F,I Coys
1st ARMORED REGIMENT	1st Bn				
	2nd Bn				
	3rd Bn				
13th ARMORED REGIMENT	1st Bn				
	2nd Bn				
	3rd Bn				

DIVISION	COMBAT COMMD 'A'	COMBAT COMMD 'B'

12th ARMORED DIVISION (NW EUROPE 1944)

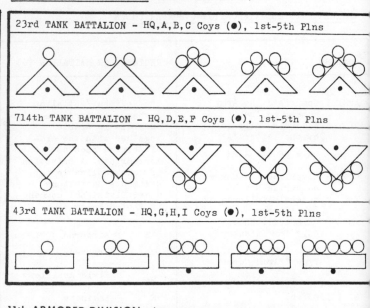

23rd TANK BATTALION - HQ,A,B,C Coys (●), 1st-5th Plns

714th TANK BATTALION - HQ,D,E,F Coys (●), 1st-5th Plns

43rd TANK BATTALION - HQ,G,H,I Coys (●), 1st-5th Plns

11th ARMORED DIVISION (NW EUROPE 1944)

42nd TANK BATTALION 3rd Coy, 1st Pln	22nd TANK BATTALION 1st Coy, 2nd Pln	41st TANK BATTALIO 2nd Coy, 4th Pln

VEHICLE SERIAL NUMBERS

Vehicle serial numbers were prefixed by the National identification 'US', 'USA' or 'US ARMY' followed by the letter 'W', indicating 'War Department'. The first numeral(s) in the serial number represented the vehicle type, the remainder representing the vehicle's sequence of issue. The suffix 'S' denoted that the vehicle was radio suppressed.

CODES :

0	trailers	7	ambulances
00	maintenance trucks	8	wheeled tractors
1	cars and sedans	9	full-track & half-track tractors
2	light trucks up to 1ton	10	kitchen trailers
	utility trucks ¾ton-1ton (1942)	20	recce trucks and buses
3	medium trucks to 1½ton	30	tanks and some specials
	light trucks 1¼ to 2tons (1942)	40	other full and half-tracks
4	trucks 2½ to 5tons	50	fire and crash trucks
	medium trucks 2½ to 4tons (1942)	60	armored Cars, commd, radio trucks
5	trucks over 5tons, prime movers	70	amphibious vehicles
	heavy trucks 5tons and over (1942)	80	tankers
6	motor cycles and combinations		

Vehicle serial numbers were coloured blue-drab, changeing to matt white during 1943. The positions were defined as :-

ambulances, panel trucks, sedans, trucks and recce trucks :- both sides of bonnet and vehicle rear, trailers :-rear, trucks without bonnets :- each end of drivers seat, combat vehicle wheeled or tracked :-both sides, front & rear

BRIDGE CLASSIFICATION NUMBERS

In the main the British system was employed, comprising a yellow disc situated at the front of the vehicle with a bridge code number, usually equivalent to vehicle loaded weight, in black numerals. Examples are as follows :-

Jeep or trailer (2), ¾ton ambulance (4), 1½ton truck (5), M8 armored car (7), 2½ton truck (10), Stuart tank (15), M18 Tank-destroyer (16), Sherman tank (30), Pershing tank (34)

RANK INSIGNIA

Consisted of a plate 6ins x 9ins, one on the front right wing or bumper and one on the rear bumper. The insignia was removed or covered when the general officer was not present. Plates were coloured red with white stars thus :-

1 star (Brigadier General), 2 stars (Major General), 3 stars (Lieut General), 4 stars (General), 5 stars (Gen.of Army)

88

INDEX TO DIVISIONS & TABLE OF COMPONENT UNITS

Infantry Division	Infantry Regts			Fld Artillery Battalions				Sigs Coy	Ord Coy	QM Coy	Recce Troop	Engineer Battalion	Medical Battalion
1	16	18	26	5	7	32	33	1	701	1	1	1	1
2	9	23	38	12	15	37	38	2	702	2	2	2	2
3	7	15	30	9	10	39	41	3	703	3	3	10	3
4	8	12	22	20	29	42	44	4	704	4	4	4	4
5	2	10	11	19	21	46	50	5	705	5	5	7	5
8	13	28	121	28	43	45	56	8	708	8	8	12	8
9	39	47	60	26	34	60	84	9	709	9	9	15	9
26	101	104	328	101	102	180	263	39	726	26	26	101	114
28	109	110	112	107	108	109	229	28	728	28	28	103	103
29	115	116	175	110	111	224	227	29	729	29	29	121	104
30	117	119	120	113	118	197	230	30	730	30	30	105	105
34	133	135	168	125	151	175	185	34	734	34	34	109	109
35	134	137	320	127	161	216	219	35	735	35	35	60	110
36	141	142	143	131	132	133	155	36	736	36	36	111	111
42	222	232	242	232	292	402	542	42	742	42	42	142	122
44	71	114	324	156	157	217	220	44	744	44	44	63	119
45	157	179	180	158	160	171	189	45	700	45	45	120	120
63	253	254	255	718	861	862	863	563	763	63	63	263	363
65	259	260	261	720	867	868	869	565	765	65	65	265	365
66	262	263	264	721	870	871	872	566	766	66	66	266	366
69	271	272	273	724	879	880	881	569	769	69	69	269	369
70	274	275	276	725	882	883	884	570	770	70	70	270	370
71	5	14	66	564	607	608	609	571	771	251	71	271	371
75	289	290	291	730	897	898	899	575	775	75	75	275	375
76	304	385	417	302	355	364	901	76	776	76	76	301	301
78	309	310	311	307	308	309	903	78	778	78	78	303	303
79	313	314	315	310	311	312	904	79	779	79	79	304	304
80	317	318	319	313	314	315	905	80	780	80	80	305	305
83	329	330	331	322	323	324	908	83	783	83	83	308	308
84	333	334	335	325	326	327	909	84	784	84	84	309	309
85	337	338	339	328	329	403	910	85	785	85	85	310	310
86	341	342	343	331	332	404	911	86	786	86	86	311	311
87	345	346	347	334	335	336	912	87	787	87	87	312	312
88	349	350	351	337	338	339	913	88	788	88	88	313	313
89	353	354	355	340	341	563	914	89	789	89	89	314	314
90	357	358	359	343	344	345	915	90	790	90	90	315	315

INDEX TO DIVISIONS & TABLE OF COMPONENT UNITS

Infantry Division	Infantry Regts			Fld Artillery Battalions				Sigs Coy	Ord Coy	QM Coy	Recce Troop	Engineer Battalion	Medical Battalion
91	361	362	363	346	347	348	916	91	791	91	91	316	316
92	365	370	371	597	598	599	600	92	792	92	92	317	317
94	301	302	376	301	356	390	919	94	794	94	94	319	319
95	377	378	379	358	359	360	920	95	795	95	95	320	320
97	303	386	387	303	365	389	922	97	797	97	97	322	322
99	393	394	395	370	371	372	924	99	799	99	99	324	324
100	397	398	399	373	374	375	925	100	800	100	100	325	325
102	405	406	407	379	380	381	927	102	802	102	102	327	327
103	409	410	411	382	383	384	928	103	803	103	103	328	328
104	413	414	415	385	386	387	929	104	804	104	104	329	329
106	422	423	424	589	590	591	592	106	806	106	106	81	331

Armored Division	Armd Infantry Battalions			Armd Fld Arty Battalions			Tank Battalions			Armd Ord Battalion	Armd Medic Battalion	Armd Engr Battalion	Cav Recce Squadron	Sigs Coy
1	6	11	14	27	68	91	1	4	13	123	47	16	81	141
2	41*	63*	67*	14	78	92	-	-	-	2	48	17	82	142
3	32*	33*	36*	54	67	391	-	-	-	3	45	23	83	143
4	10	51	53	22	66	94	8	35	37	126	4	24	25	144
5	15	46	47	47	71	95	10	34	81	127	75	22	85	145
6	9	44	50	128	212	231	15	68	69	128	76	25	86	146
7	23	38	48	434	440	489	17	31	40	129	77	33	87	147
8	7	49	58	398	399	405	18	36	80	130	78	53	88	148
9	27	52	60	3	16	73	2	14	19	131	2	9	89	149
10	20	54	61	419	420	423	3	11	21	132	80	55	90	150
11	21	55	63	490	491	492	22	41	42	133	81	56	41	151
12	17	56	66	493	494	495	23	43	714	134	82	119	92	152
13	16	59	67	496	497	498	24	45	46	135	83	124	93	153
14	19	62	68	499	500	501	25	47	48	136	84	125	94	154
16	18	64	69	393	396	397	5	16	26	137	216	216	23	156
20	8	65	70	412	413	414	9	20	27	138	220	220	30	160

* Armored Regiments - 2nd & 3rd Armd Divns did not change from Heavy Armd Organisation with T/O & E Sept 1943

A'Borne Divn	Infantry Regiments				Artillery Bns				AA Bn	Para Maint Coy	Sigs Coy	Ord Coy	Qm Coy	Engineer Bn	Medical Coy
	Glider		Para		Glider		Para								
13th	88	326	515	517	676	677	458	460	153	13	513	713	409	129	129
17th	193	194	507	513	680	681	464	466	155	17	517	717	411	139	224
82nd	325	-	504	505	319	320	376	456	80	82	82	782	407	307	307
101st	327	401	502	506	321	907	377	463	101	101	801	426	426	326	326

SELECT BIBLIOGRAPHY

US Army Order of Battle- N.Africa & Europe- 1943-45	Madjez, W.Victor	Game Publishing
US Army Handbook 1939-45	Forty, George	Ian Allen
Operation Dragoon	Breuer, William B.	Airlife
US Armor Camouflage & Markings 1917-45	Zaloga, Steven J	Osprey-Vanguard 39
World War 2 Military Vehicle Markings	Wise, Terence	Patrick Stevens
Armor, Camouflage & Markings- N.Africa 1940-43	Bradford, George R.	Arms & Armour Press
British & American Tanks of World War 2	Chamberlain P. & Ellis C.	Arms & Armour Press
Illustrated Encyclopedia of Military Vehicles	Hogg, Ian V. & Weeks J.	New Burlington Books

Note: Further information on US Tanks in British Service may be found in Datafile 1 'British Tanks & Formations 1939-45